SKILLS
FOR
CAMPING

MONTIE ROLAND

CONTENTS

PROLOGUE 5
ONE: LANTERNS: ELECTRIC VS. PROPANE 9
TWO: CHOOSING A KNIFE 17
THREE: TYPES OF CAMPERS 25
FOUR: MOVING THE COMFORTS OF HOME 31
FIVE: THE HANDY DANDY UTILITY TRAILER 35
SIX: PACKING YOUR CAR 45
SEVEN: WATER FOR DRINKING 51
EIGHT: SHOWERS AND CAMP HYGIENE 61
NINE: PITCH YOUR TENT 73
TEN: CAMP KITCHEN 85
ELEVEN: FIRST AID 97
TWELVE: HIKING 109
THIRTEEN: BEAUTY FROM ADVERSITY 125
FOURTEEN: PLANNING FOR EXPECTATIONS AND EXPERIENCES 133
FIFTEEN: CAMPING AT THE JEEP JAMBOREE 145
SIXTEEN: PHYSICAL FITNESS IMPROVES CAMPING EXPERIENCE 155
SEVENTEEN: CAMPING AT DIFFERENT STAGES OF LIFE 161
EIGHTEEN: CAMPING WITH A DOG 169

SKILLS FOR CAMPING

Copyright © 2019, Montie Roland

All rights reserved. Reproduction in part or in whole is strictly forbidden without the express written consent of the publisher.

Cover and interior design by Roseanna White Designs
Cover illustrations from Shutterstock

ISBNS: 978-1-7335969-4-7 (print)
           978-1-7335969-3-0` (digital)

PROLOGUE

The word "camping" inspires smiles in many people. My goal is to show you how to create memorable family experiences in the woods. First off, I'd like to thank you for buying this book. If you're about to embark on your first camping trip then forge ahead and let me share what I've learned over the years. On the other hand, if you've camped a few times and are looking for tips on how to be more efficient and accomplished in your future trips, then read on. I always say *knowledge weighs nothing*. My hope is that you'll find yourself better informed and prepared after reading this book.

Allow me to share a little about myself. As a graduate of North Carolina State University, my day job is mechanical engineering specializing in new product development. I was raised in Asheville, NC, where I earned my Eagle Scout award. Growing up, our home was located only a few miles from the Blue Ridge Parkway, so I had many blessed opportunities to spend time outside. My childhood was an exceptional gateway to outdoor adventure for an inquisitive kid with tons of time and a vivid imagination.

As an avid outdoor enthusiast, I'd say my happy place is being in the woods. Over the years, I've had the opportunity to camp in North Carolina, Virginia, and New Mexico. The trip to New Mexico was a ninety mile backpacking trip to Philmont, the famous Boy Scout reservation. These rich experiences have molded me into the man I am today.

My wife and I own land in the mountains near Hot Springs, NC, where we hope to build a cabin sometime over the next couple of years. Until then, Connie and I enjoy tent camping there several times a year.

I have found that camping is a great way to enjoy nature while keeping your trips inexpensive. When you camp, you save money, which allows you to spread your funds over more excursions and spend more time outdoors—which is a win-win for everybody involved! Just like everyone else who works nine-to-five, I struggle with my work life balance. Throw in family and responsibilities at home, you quickly realize you must carve out time to do what you enjoy.

If you haven't read my prior book, *Family Camping* (Montie's Guide to Camping, Book One), feel free to grab that in either Kindle or print format. Here's a quick blurb:

> Written for beginner to semi-seasoned outdoor-enthusiasts, this book will not only

teach you how to camp but show you what to expect, how to plan activities, and how to create traditions. The word "camping" inspires smiles in many people. Learn how to escape your daily life and create memorable family experiences in the woods.

This book, *Skills for Camping* (Montie's Guide to Camping, Book Two), will cover a lot of skills and topics that apply to camping in your area and at different stages of life. Camping is a great experience for your family. Hopefully this book helps you escape your daily life and enjoy the outdoors!

ONE

LANTERNS: ELECTRIC VS. PROPANE

A lantern is very handy for general use. You can either sit it on the table or hang it from somewhere. A good place to hang it is the shelter where you set up your kitchen. Sometimes we'll set up a kitchen underneath a permanent shelter, other times we use a ten-by-ten pop-up shelter. Either way, the shelter is used to provide protection from the sun and the rain.

For years, I have attached a piece of copper wire at the peak of our pop-up kitchen shelter where I hang our lantern. It brings the lantern low enough so you can turn it on and off, and adjust the light. I have a Coleman lantern that uses a one pound propane tank. We've hauled that lantern all around, and it still works great. If you go camping a lot, you'll probably end up with a propane one. But, let's go over the pros and cons in case you've never purchased or used a lantern.

SOLAR, ELECTRIC, AND BATTERY POWERED LANTERNS

Solar powered has batteries plus a solar cell; otherwise you couldn't store the power. There are some really cool designs where they put out a very diffuse light. Since they are solar, the battery charges during the day and it runs down at night. That is nice because you don't have to carry batteries around, and you won't get to your campsite and discover your batteries are dead. On the other hand, if you set up camp late in the day, or if it was cloudy, then the lantern didn't charge so you may be without light. The benefit of a battery powered unit is you can turn it on and off.

Inflatable, solar powered lantern works great in the tent

If you're going for a single night of camping with a battery powered lantern, check to make sure your batteries are fresh. You can also use rechargeable batteries in them, but they're usually going to get slightly dimmer as the battery power decreases.

There are also true electric lanterns that you connect to an electrical outlet to charge just like your phone. Of course, this assumes you have access to electricity during your camping trip.

One big advantage these lanterns have over propane

is that you can set them anywhere. A propane lantern can't be bumped as it might tip over and start a fire which is why I hang ours from a copper wire.

Inside your tent you'll want to use either electric or solar light. You can hang your flashlight, or get an inflatable solar lantern that you can squish down when you're done. Or, if you've got plenty of room, they have some that don't deflate. Camping solar lights put out a nice diffuse light, enough for you to change your clothes, get in your sleeping bag; then you charge it the next day. I think they are a great light for when you can't have an open flame.

CHEMICAL LANTERNS

I'm not really hip on the chemical because they're not very bright—in this case I'm referring to glow sticks. The nice thing with glow sticks, though, is they're tiny. If you are out of space and you need something to give you some minimal light, you can go with the glow stick. They do glow for a long time. Note that, when you are done with them, you throw away a bunch of plastic and a lot of chemicals.

PROPANE LANTERNS

Fuel powered is nice because it emits a lot of light. You can run lantersn a long time off propane. One of those cylinders can lasts a number of camping trips. They make a soft hissing sound so you know propane's coming out. You light them, they stay lit, and weather doesn't bother them.

One downside is you need to bring extra mantles, because they get brittle, and sooner or later the mantle will fall into a thousand pieces. A mantle is the little cloth bag tied to the port where the gas comes out. Also, I wouldn't suggest sitting a propane lantern on a table because it's too easily bumped. You need to find somewhere safe to hang the propane lantern from. Don't forget, you never want to have *any* kind of open flame inside a tent. If your tent catches on fire, you're in a world of hurt.

The upside is they're not expensive, they last for years, they put out a lot of light, and they are easy to light. Also, they work in a wide variety of temperatures. I wouldn't leave it out in the pouring rain but underneath an awning where's there's incidental

Propane lantern makes night time tasks easier

raindrops is fine. They have been proven over decades; in fact the one I own is at least twenty-five years old.

I recommend keeping the box or case your lantern comes in. In fact, if you are purchasing a gas lantern, spring for the extra few dollars and get one that comes in a case. When storing or transporting the lantern, make sure the propane tank is disconnected as you don't want it accidentally turning on in transit. And make sure not to store propane inside your home.

FLASHLIGHT

I think it's a sound idea for everyone in your group to have their own flashlight. You can spend a lot or a little on a flashlight, that's up to you.

One type of flashlight you can purchase uses the F-Cell lantern batteries, which last a long time and put out a lot of light. Generally, when you have to replace the battery, the batteries are more expensive than the flashlight. They're easy for small hands to carry and keep up with. They're inexpensive, less than ten dollars each. And when you're done you can stick it in the house and use it for an emergency light.

Another option is a smaller flashlight. One advantage is it fits in your pocket easily. The downside of the smaller flashlight is that it's easier to lose and has less run time because the battery capacity is smaller.

When you look at a flashlight, consider what battery

you're going to use. There are tactical flashlights out there that use CR 123 batteries. Novelty flashlights use little coin cells. The CR 123's have the lifespan of a double A, they're more expensive, and they're not as common as a double A battery. So, if you run into a store somewhere you may not be able to replace them. They're popular in a lot of military and tactical applications. But for a camping flashlight, I'd encourage you to have a flashlight with double A batteries since they are one of the most common batteries on the planet. You can replace them at any gas station.

Be cautious because you can spend a lot of money on a flashlight. The tactical flashlights are spectacular and are extremely bright, except most of the time you don't need something so fancy. A five dollar flashlight from Home Depot is probably going to work just fine. The one thing to keep in mind is when you have a hundred dollar flashlight, generally it's higher quality. A five dollar flashlight will be lower quality. All that means is once you get outside and bang it around in your pocket, or in your car, or you drop it on rocks a few times—the lower quality one will fail a lot sooner than the more expensive one. Somewhere in there is a happy medium. Consider where you are going and the ages of your children and figure out what will work best for you.

From a functional standpoint, you want something to give you enough light, usually to go from one end of the campground to the other, or check on a flat tire, or something like that. It's not a high-performance need. And keep a spare flashlight as well as spare batteries.

It's always a good idea to have flashlights around the house. When the power goes off, you might be in a room that's inconvenient to get to the flashlight from. I also think it's really smart for kids to have a flashlight in front of their beds, so if the power goes off or they need to find you, they're not walking through the house in the dark. If it's your first camping trip, get something that's high enough quality to last for your trip. After your excursion, consider repurposing the flashlight for use in your home.

TWO

CHOOSING A KNIFE

When you're out camping, having a pocket knife is handy. You'll need it for different tasks—to cut a piece of rope, to cut a stick, open a box. In an emergency, a pocket knife can be a lifesaver. I'd encourage you to keep a knife with you at all times.

DIFFERENT KINDS OF KNIVES

A knife is something that has a blade that you can cut with. I don't mean swords or daggers or things like that. The blade should be four inches or shorter.

A knife has a hand grip, where your hand holds the knife. If the knife folds, like a pocket knife, the sides of the handle are called scales. A folding knife when folded will be from three to five inches long.

The other type of knife is a fixed blade knife. A fixed blade doesn't fold and has a sheath that the blade goes into to protect the user from the knife when it's not in use. Your kitchen knife is a fixed blade knife. Fixed blade knives can be really cool. Having a KA-BAR is really nice—this is the giant fighting knife the Marines carry. They're handy, they're tough; but they're three hundred bucks. I'm going to make the argument that, while I like fixed blade knives and while Montie Gear makes a high quality fixed blade knife, most of the time I end up carrying a folding knife more because of legalities and it's also easier to fit in my pocket. You should put a fixed blade knife back in the sheath when not in use.

There are fairly long folding blade knives that fit in your pocket, but they are still shorter than your cell phone when folded. To have the same length fixed blade knife, you've got this giant knife on your belt.

MAKE SURE WHAT YOU CARRY IS LEGAL WHERE YOU ARE

You'll need to check in your state about the requirements for different types of knives. In some states there may be a limit to the length of blade you are allowed to carry in say a college campus or a school. This varies by jurisdiction in some cities, too. Generally, there's a limit of blade length when concealed. Check your local and state and regional laws, but generally you can carry a sword at your waist if it's in the open. If you conceal a sword it may fall under a totally different set of laws. Always make sure to obey the knife laws.

In North Carolina, you can conceal a fixed blade knife up to a certain length, I believe it's three and a half inches; beyond that, it needs to be out in the open. Some of these laws aren't necessarily intuitive. You can rest assured that the law came about because something happened, and someone ended up doing something stupid and now we have a law. In North Carolina, there are a different set of standards applied to a folding knife or a fixed blade. You'll find in some localities you can have a folding knife where the blade is much longer than the blade on a fixed knife. Generally, in a lot of places, when you're knife blade is under three-and-a-half inches you can carry a folding knife without a problem. There's definitely a prejudice against fixed blade knives, check the local laws.

There are limitations to places you can carry a knife. You'll see government buildings with no weapons signs, so you can't carry a knife into the building.

MY SUGGESTION

Buy a folding blade knife and then you can carry it just about anywhere. They run from five dollars at the flea market or up to how much you want to spend on Amazon. Generally, there's a sweet spot. I'll say between seventy to a hundred and fifty dollars. I have found cheaper ones, except the steel isn't as good so it won't hold an edge as well and won't last as long. But if it's for a camping trip, it's probably okay. Keep in mind that you may end up with that knife for the rest of your life, or until you lose it.

There's also a category of what people will call pocket knives. My only problem with a pocket knife is that a lot of them don't lock the blade in the open position. My preference is a folding knife that locks when it opens. That way the knife doesn't collapse on your fingers and cut you while you're using it. Now granted, my grandfather carried a pocket knife, and my dad carries one. My grandfather was in his seventies when he died, and my dad's eighty-eight and neither had a lot of scars on their fingers. If you're new to knives I feel you should purchase one with the locking safety feature. I've got a SOG knife that I like a lot. There are Benchmade knives that are wonderful. There are many well-made folding knives available.

Fixed blade Montie Gear Knife

Montie Gear makes a really great fixed blade knife! I know this is a shameless advertisement, but I'm proud of the knife we make and it works really, really well in a camping or backpacking environment.

Ask yourself if this is something you can use as an everyday carry knife. Multiple uses out of the same equipment make it cost-effective. You can use the knife beyond the campsite because it's a tool; the more familiar you become with that tool, the better you can use that tool when you're camping, and you'll be safer.

THE KNIFE BLADE

The steel and how it is ground affects how well the knife blade will hold and take an edge. There are many different opinions on the way to grind these blades, as well as the different types of steels.

Generally, a better knife is made of a higher quality and more exotic steel. All the steel options have different pluses and minuses. Some of them will develop a patina and that means it will slowly rust. Even if you keep oiling it, one day it will have a kind of brown-black color. It may look fine as long as you keep it oiled. The ones that develop patina will end up with splotches on them if not oiled.

A lot of the blades nowadays are stainless or tool steel. A tool steel one needs to be oiled regularly. Stainless steel ones won't need as much work to keep looking nice.

I typically avoid buying knives with serrations because serrated edges on the blade are difficult to sharpen, which I feel limits the lifetime of the knife.

DO YOU LOSE BELONGINGS OR KEEP THEM FOREVER?

I'll argue people fall into two categories, either you lose it before it wears out or you wear it out before you lose it. If you're in the latter group, you'll carry the knife you buy forever—so whatever you purchase is a good buy. If you tend to lose belongings, then be cost-effective and consider buying a more economical knife.

SHARPEN AND OIL

A dull knife is much more dangerous than a sharp knife. If you keep your knife sharp, it's a point of pride. It'll do its job better and will be less likely to slip and cut you. When it's sharp you don't have to apply as much pressure. When it's dull, you have to apply a lot more pressure, and that's often when a knife slips, and then you lose control and cut yourself, or somebody else. So, if you've got a sharp one, it takes a fraction of the amount of pressure and you're less likely to injure yourself.

Many times when you sharpen your knife, you're going to oil it as well because it's part of the sharpening process. Stainless steel doesn't need oiling as often, every other blade does. You don't want to cut food with your folding knife because it's been in your pocket and you have used it for many things that may not be compatible with sanitary food. Keep a separate knife for cooking and eating.

If you're lost in a survival situation, go ahead and use your pocket knife to eat with, but not in a normal situation.

WRAP UP

There are fixed blades, folding knives, and pocketknives. If you are only going to own one knife then you'll want to stay away from fixed blades because they're just not as easy to carry and pocket knives don't lock. If this is the only knife you're going to own, get yourself a nice big folding knife. Check your local and state laws to make sure it's not going to cause a problem. And check blade length versus any concealed carry laws.

Consider what the steel blades are made from and compare the quality and character of the knife with your needs and budget. If you've got plenty of budget, we have some really nice Montie Gear knives. They're fixed blade and a little over three inches long, so in most places you can carry those without a problem. Not only are they really nice, they're even a little bit sexy—a little commercial there. Learn how to sharpen your knife and keep it sharp.

Finally, there are tons of videos on the web about how to select a knife, with different levels of purists. Some people from "Hey, this is a great knife" to people who have very exacting requirements. Feel free to look into this a little more if you need.

A dull knife is much more dangerous than a sharp knife. If you keep your knife sharp, it's a point of pride; it'll do its job better and you're less likely to cut yourself.

THREE

TYPES OF CAMPERS

Instead of camping in a tent, consider a trailer of some sort.

POP-UP TRAILERS

For a pop-up camper, I'm going to make the argument that it takes the same amount of time to pitch a tent as it does to get a pop-up in place. However, once in place, you are good to go. Pop-ups can have kitchens, so it's a little different experience. A big positive with the smaller campers is the ability to tow them with a car or SUV.

TEARDROP TRAILERS

A teardrop is a trailer that's usually shaped kind of like a teardrop on its side. Most cars can easily tow them and there is enough room to sleep inside. A lot of times it'll have a kitchen space on one end, and you can store some of

SKILLS FOR CAMPING

your gear inside while traveling. The positive thing is you don't have to pitch a tent. You're also up off the ground, which means you're climbing into a bed that's at the normal height, not low. Some of them have air-conditioning and heat. If you've got power at your campsite, then you plug in and sleep in comfort off the ground in your teardrop. Also, you can store your gear safely inside the teardrop trailer while you are away having adventures during the day.

Our teardrop camper

There are also extra large teardrop style trailers that have more room for gear. You may be able to rent a small camping trailer in your area, which is a good way to enjoy the experience without having to buy an expensive tear drop or pop-up trailer.

Teardrops are available in traditional, off-road, and four-wheel-drive configurations. Generally a four-wheel drive trailer has several things going for it. The first is bigger tires. Ideally, they are the same size as your four-wheel-drive. On my Jeep, I run thirty-five inch tires on fifteen inch rims. So it'd be really nice to have a camping trailer with thirty-five inch tires. One advantage is that as you're going over obstacles, your trailer has a similar capability of crossing over rocks, ditches, what have you, because the tire size is the same. I don't want to get too far into this issue but basically as tires get smaller, the ease of going over a given obstacle becomes more difficult because of where the obstruct strikes the tire. The other nice thing is you only need one spare, you can use the same spare on your tow rig, your Jeep or your other four-wheel drive; or you can use that spare on your trailer.

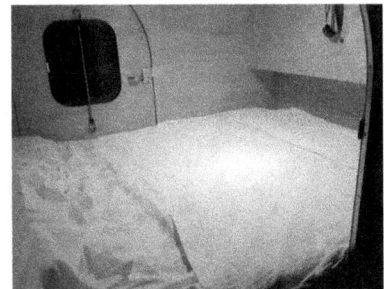
Inside our teardrop camper - very simple

This year Connie and I bought a teardrop camper to make those quick weekend trips easier. Hopefully that means we can make more of them. Living in North Carolina gives us lots of places to go within a 3-4 hour drive. Hunting season has also just started here, so Saturday mornings have become prime time to spend time in a tree stand chasing that elusive monster buck. This Saturday, the plan is to hike Mount Mitchell (highest peak on the East) before the winter weather arrives.

ROOFTOP TENT TRAILERS

There are also off-road trailers with expanding tents that sit on the top of the trailer. They are called rooftop tents and are available for vehicles like Jeep Wranglers, Land Rovers, and Toyota 4Runners. These are gaining in popularity with the Overlanding groups, as they're handy in places where you may not be guaranteed a place to camp, say out in the desert or someplace it may be more difficult to find a spot to pitch your tent. The negative is that you're towing a trailer behind you and when you arrive at the campsite you still have to open up a tent. On the flip side, you are able to sleep up off the ground.

TREND IS MOVING TO OVERLANDING

One of the things you'll see if you start looking at camping stuff is a new genre that's come up over the last few years. If you enjoy camping, this may be the direction you head in. The concept came from Australia where a lot of times they'll go "overlanding," which is where you take a trailer designed to go behind your four-wheel drive. In Australia, there are thousands and thousands of miles of open spaces—a lot of high desert. So people will go hundreds of miles into the woods and take what they need with them. If you take a four-wheel drive vehicle, there's a limit to how much gear you can take.

Camping in a van

Also, sometimes it's difficult to stop at a place where you have room to actually set up camp.

I'm not suggesting in any way, shape or form, for you to rush out and equip your vehicle for overlanding. That's a significant amount of money to spend to just give it a try. I'll make the argument that a couple of small footprint tents and you can generally find a place to set it. So, in my mind it's a lower priority. If it's something you want to do at some point, go ahead and embrace it. But I think a lot of times it's just not where you want to start your camping experience, because you might not like it and then you've purchased a lot of specialized, expensive equipment you're not going to use.

Though some people have the funds and the drive to jump in with both feet, my thought is to start simple and have a good time. I would encourage you to look towards doing a lot of this stuff from the onset on a budget, so you can enjoy it without spending too much money. Later on you can improve pieces of equipment, kind of like the Dirt Everyday philosophy. Take what you've got; don't spend a whole lot of money in the beginning; go out; enjoy it. And then go from there.

HOW CONNIE AND I OVERLAND

A lot of these overland vehicles also get taken on what I'll call "day four-wheeling," which is what we do. Our Jeep Wrangler gets used for a Jeep Jamboree or we'll go four-wheeling on a Saturday for a few hours and drive back. The overlanding part is kind of a nifty way to extend the use of your vehicle. We have a two-door TJ Jeep Wrangler and there's almost no storage space. They're awesome vehicles, awesome, awesome vehicles. Except storage just wasn't high on priority when they were designed.

When you hear people talking about overlanding, it's this cool subset of RV camping/four-wheeling. I guess that's maybe the best way to describe it—where the RV meets the four-wheel drive. And that's kind of a neat thing.

A SPARE TIRE FOR YOUR TRAILER

It may be the trailer configuration you're looking at doesn't support the same size tire as your vehicle. In that case, you'll need to carry a spare for your vehicle and one for your trailer.

TOWING A TRAILER

Towing a trailer makes a lot of sense. When you're camping, it makes even more sense because you've got gear you need to take with you.

FOUR

MOVING THE COMFORTS OF HOME

Many people find it easier to camp when they bring the comforts of home. The problem is that some of those items may be large and bulky to transport in a car. If you are travelling with two adults and one child in an SUV, you can probably manage to pack all belongings into your vehicle, but if you need more space, you might want to consider a small trailer or a cargo carrier basket.

ROOFTOP CARGO CARRIER

If you have an SUV, there's a good chance you've got cargo rails on the top where the carrier straps down to those rails. There are ones that work with sedans, cars as well. If you don't have rails on the top of your vehicle, you may need to purchase something like a Thule roof rack. It's definitely an expensive way to gain a few cubic feet of storage, but it works. You might spend five hundred bucks to put that together. Sometimes they have toppers that are held down with straps or pads so you don't have to have the rails. All these options have pluses and minuses.

One of the first times our family camped together, you can see the bike rack and all the boxes

We've got one of those boxes. We used it a few times for trips when we had the minivan, and unfortunately it spent the next ten years on the top shelf basically in storage because we just don't have a need for it.

CARGO CARRIER BASKET

You can add storage to the back of your car by connecting a basket cargo carrier directly to the hitch. These baskets are usually about the width of the car; aluminum or steel; and they slide into the receiver of the trailer hitch. It's a great place to put anything that can get wet, like a cooler.

I've seen these baskets at Harbor Freight for between eighty to two hundred and fifty dollars.

LIGHT TRAILER

If you're towing the trailer behind your car, even if

you don't have much weight in the trailer, there's still more drag from the wind. That means your car's working harder which means you need to drive slower than usual. All this translates to the transmission getting hotter. Since heat is the enemy of your transmission, be careful!

YOU MAY NEED A TRAILER HITCH

If you use a cargo carrier basket, small utility, or light trailer you will need a trailer hitch. If you don't already have one, purchase a trailer hitch. Most cars and definitely almost all SUVs and trucks accept one. Different cars have different towing recommendations; you can look up the manufacturer rating for your particular vehicle.

Most of the trailers you would use for camping either use a 1-7/8 or 2-inch ball. It is very important to use the correct ball. Check the top of the trailer coupler for the size of the ball diameter required.

Note that the receiver tube size of the trailer hitch on a car will be a smaller diameter, usually one and a quarter. But, since most items in the towing world are two inches, you can purchase an adapter that increases it to two inches. The reason why they put the smaller receiver on cars is they weren't meant to pull heavy trailers.

TRANSPORTING BIKES

When you have your hitch for your car, it's a convenient way to transport bikes. You can plug your bike rack into the hitch. That's a very handy thing, especially with kids, because now you don't have to cram the bikes in the car. You just throw them on and go for a day ride. Optionally, you can get an adapter that allows you to use your bike rack and your trailer. It extends the hitch out. It does limit the amount of cargo you can haul in your trailer but that gives you another option which is a really nice way to store your bikes and tow your trailer.

SMALL UTILITY TRAILER

If you have a small trailer, maybe a four-by-eight, or a five-by-eight, you will use it for things other than camping. They're really nice for camping because they give you room to put everything in the trailer, and you don't have to pack everything so tight in the car.

Obviously if you have a giant pickup truck, a lot of stuff can go in the bed so you may not have space constraints. Or perhaps you have an Expedition or one of those extra-large SUVs, then maybe this doesn't really apply. But for the rest of us who have a small SUV all the way down to a car, then one of the above options may be the only way to transport some of these creature comforts with you.

Having this additional space will also help when departing the camp site because you won't need to pack so tightly and efficiently.

FIVE

THE HANDY DANDY UTILITY TRAILER

When you organize your camping gear into several different boxes, you can find items quickly. The last thing you want is to dig for something in the bottom of a giant box.

NOT EVERYTHING FITS IN YOUR VEHICLE

Unfortunately, boxes you've chosen don't always match up with the space you have available in your vehicle. So, for example you may have a car or a small SUV or even a big SUV and a lot of people. Perhaps the waterproof box you plan to leave outside at the campsite doesn't fit well with all the other stuff you packed. One solution is to buy a small trailer to haul items that can get wet, because sooner or later it will rain on you. Items in

SKILLS FOR CAMPING

Packed up and ready to go

the trailer should be able to get wet or are in water resistant containers.

I am not suggesting you go out and purchase a trailer for your first camping trip. The first trip should be simple and local. If you find you enjoy camping and want to take longer trips, hauling a trailer will be appealing.

We have owned a pickup, SUVs, and cars over the years and taken camping trips with all of them. The easiest combination for us has been an SUV with a trailer. The trailer and SUV combination gives you the option for easier packing and more space while having seats for everyone and dry, lockable storage in the SUV I think it is much easier to tow the trailer than use our roof top carrier on the SUV. You can make whatever vehicle you have work. If you are completely out of space then consider adding a receiver hitch to your vehicle and towing a small trailer, buying a used roof top carrier, or using a receiver hitch mounted basket. There are plenty of options, but probably you can make the vehicle you have now work without any modifications or any additional equipment. If you have a large family, another option is to just drive two vehicles.

A RECEIVER HITCH FOR CARS

When you purchase a vehicle, you will often be offered the receiver hitch option from the factory as part of a towing package. Some of the towing packages include an oil cooler, which keeps the transmission cooler. You can add a receiver hitch to most cars which is not expensive and gives you a lot more options for cargo on trips. The cost is about one hundred twenty-five to two hundred fifty dollars. It's a fairly simple installation on most cars, and something you can do in your driveway.

If you are towing a small utility trailer, then you probably won't need electric brakes on the trailer and an electric brake interface in the car. All you will need is the receiver hitch.

CONSIDER A SMALL TRAILER

A small trailer, when not overloaded, can be towed behind a variety of vehicles. Keep in mind whenever you tow a trailer, your transmission and the trailer tire capacity are always the weak links. Research how much weight your vehicle can tow and the maximum weight and speed of the trailer. Many trailers also require a much higher tire pressure than a car tire. The sidewall of the tire displays the load capacity and the required pressure.

My experiences with five-by-eight or smaller is that with the trailer unloaded, you can pretty effortlessly

SKILLS FOR CAMPING

unhook and move it around. Any bigger than five-by-eight and easily moving the trailer becomes a challenge.

Avoid the temptation to purchase a large trailer unless you have a heavier duty vehicle for towing and you are up to dealing with it.

BIGGER TRAILERS ARE MORE DIFFICULT TO MANAGE

If your trailer is larger than five-by-eight, or five-by-eight with metal sides, it can be difficult to move by hand. Some trailers have an extra wheel at the front, which folds down to support the weight at the tongue. This allows you to roll the trailer on smooth surfaces without having to support the weight at the tongue. If you don't have the wheel at the tongue, it may be necessary to move the trailer with the tow vehicle because it is too heavy to move by hand. Lighter trailers (when unloaded) are much easier to move by hand. These are considerations to keep in mind when purchasing a trailer.

HOW TO STORE THE TRAILER

Some trailers allow you to store them in a vertical position. Depending on your property, that may be a good option. If you have a large garage, but no yard space, then a storable trailer is a nice choice. Some have wheels that fold flat. One of the challenges in suburban life is there's nowhere to put one. You may have restrictive covenants; or you may have difficulties storing a trailer on your property. Sometimes if the item can't be viewed from the road, then it's not covered by restrictive covenants.

FLAT TIRE?

You have options if your trailer has a flat tire. One is to plan to purchase one wherever you have a flat. That may or may not be easy depending on the trailer bolt pattern. The other option is to purchase a spare ahead of time to be prepared.

There are a bunch of different wheel and tire combinations for trailers, with different loads and so forth. Some are more common than others. I've got a five-by-eight trailer with a very uncommon bolt pattern. So, if I replace a tire, I have to order it, which would be difficult to do on the road. Keep that in mind, because a trailer with a standard tire size can be found at Walmart, Tractor Supply, Northern Tool.

TRAILER TIRE SIZE

Generally you want to have a larger tire so you can drive at a normal speed. The really small trailer tires don't allow you to tow at seventy miles an hour. The larger the tire size, the number of RPMs the wheel has to make decreases, so it rotates more like a car tire.

The small trailer tires can't tow past fifty-five miles an hour because you could destroy them, especially when there is weight on them. Generally, you want a larger tire;

a thirteen to fifteen-inch tire, which will be similar to a car tire. This size tire will allow you to travel with traffic, as most highways have a speed limit of sixty-five or seventy miles-per-hour.

Make sure you check out your tire rating. Also, make sure you have a lug wrench that fits your trailer.

TRAILER SIDES, PERMANENT OR TEMPORARY

Having sides on your trailer makes it easier to load. Trailers either have permanently welded on or removable wooden sides. Usually the wood side one's a little lighter and has the flexibility of removable sides if you need access to the side or the front of the trailer for some reason.

Trailers are handy to have outside of camping. Anything from moving a sofa for a buddy, or a table you just bought at an antique store, maybe mulch in the spring. They are a good investment beyond this immediate camping use. A trailer extends the cargo space for your SUV or your car, and it's something you can hook up quickly and go.

SAFETY CHAINS

Connect the trailer correctly and always use safety chains. A safety chain will save your butt. Use something to lock the trailer after you connect the hitch. There's going to be a lever arm that comes down with a hole in it. Make sure there is a lock or bolt or something to keep the arm from coming off the hitch.

I have a couple of tricks to lock the trailer in place. One is to use a nylon bolt and nut to run through the hole to lock

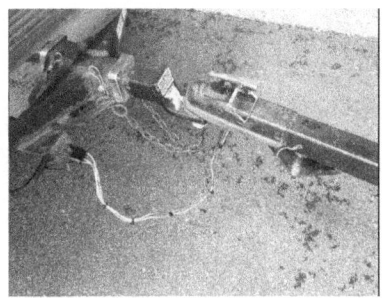

Always double check the connections - chain, ball, and lights

the trailer tongue onto the ball. Those don't back out. A metal bolt will want to back out over time, but the nylon bolt with a nylon nut won't. Another option is to use a combination lock or padlock, that way no one will go off with your trailer, and you know it's not going to fall off because it's locked. Both these options give you security and peace of mind. Trust me, having a trailer come off the ball at fifty-five miles an hour would be a really bad thing.

ORGANIZING CAMPING GEAR IN A TRAILER

Start laying out your boxes or however you plan to carry your materials to the campsite. Take those items and lay them out in logical groupings. For example, you've got things like a lantern, a Kelty pot, your cooking gear, in one box; another box is food; another box could be your dry clothes or your bedding. So now start laying out these boxes by function.

Trailer makes hauling gear easy

Since you're not as constrained by the space within your vehicle, you can pack more for how you're going to use your equipment at the campsite. The goal is when I pull my boxes off the trailer, they will already be organized and ready for use. So, the hundred times you go in and out of that box you're not having to dig through stuff to look for one thing that settled to the bottom of the container.

Having a trailer is a handy thing if you have room for it. If you don't, we already talked about the car topper and the basket hitch. I recommend organizing your items the same way no matter what tool you use to bring them to the camp site.

WHERE TO PURCHASE A TRAILER

There are many sources for trailers. A trailer has a certain amount of utility, no matter how rough a shape it's in. A new three-by-four trailer from somewhere like Northern Tool might be about eight hundred bucks, and the one you find used down the street might be four hundred and in horrible shape. Figure out your budget and what effort you're willing to put into it.

Keep in mind, wooden trailer floorboards eventually

rot. So, you might purchase one for three hundred bucks and have to put a day of work into cleaning it up and replacing the flooring. If you do have to replace the flooring, I recommend using marine-grade plywood, pressure-treated wood, or wood you plan to paint or stain as the trailer is out in the elements. Because it's exposed to the weather, eventually you're going to have to replace decking on a used trailer.

Let me remind you again to keep the first camping trip easy. After a successful first outing, if you decide to go again for a week, think about getting a trailer, especially if you have storage room and you'll use it for other things. If you do much in your yard, or have friends who move, or need to pick up a large item you've purchased, a trailer comes in handy.

SIX

PACKING YOUR CAR

How you pack and what you bring is vitally important to a successful camping trip. If you bring too much, then there is more to manage and the extra items get in the way. And let's be honest, whatever type of vehicle you have doesn't have that much spare space.

CREATURE COMFORTS CAN BE A MUST

On the other hand, there are crucial items, like your wife's pillow or your daughter's favorite teddy bear, which must be there. It's easy to want to take everything, but those creature comforts from home will make the weekend so much more enjoyable for everyone involved.

CONSIDER YOUR LOCALE

What you need truly depends on where you are going and for how long. If you're going to a remote wilderness area, then you must think through the equipment you'll need. But, many of the places you camp will be right down the street from grocery stores and restaurants. Perhaps there's beauty and simplicity in that. Maybe you don't cook every meal; maybe you cook dinners and eat out all others. Do what works for you and your family.

PLAN FOOD NEEDS CAREFULLY

I talked earlier about planning meals. If I am going on a hunting trip, I'll eat dinner on the way to the site and bring a precooked breakfast with me so that I don't have to start a fire in the morning. Not only does that makes things simpler, it also requires less kitchen equipment.

When I'm camping with my family, I get up early and start a fire and cook a big breakfast because its tradition and I love to do it. I may have to bring more food and cooking accouterments, but for those precious moments I'd do anything.

Sometimes simpler is better. Consider this question: what do you truly need?

A WELL-ORGANIZED CAR MAKES FOR A HAPPIER TRIP

If you throw everything in the back of your car, with no thought to organization, I can pretty much guarantee you will have a miserable trip. You will sort through that pile of stuff the whole time you're gone, wasting time and energy. You're never going to feel comfortable because

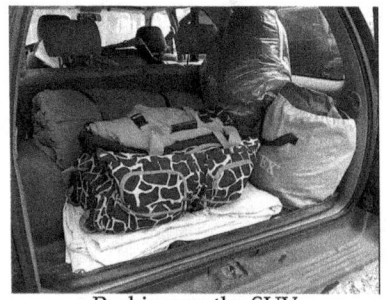
Packing up the SUV

you can't find what you are looking for.

Think of your car as a box that's filled with boxes that are filled with boxes. Organize like things together. Consider labeling containers. For example, I've got some kitchen boxes that fold open and make it really easy and quick to grab a fork. Because, if it takes you five minutes to locate a fork and a napkin, that's going to be a really long weekend. The more organized you are, the less you'll bring and the quicker you'll pack and unpack, leaving more time for fun activities.

THINK BOY SCOUT ORGANIZATION

Think of the Boy Scout concept of packing—a bag, a mini bag, a box, a mini box. That's one of the things we were taught was that your pack is a bag of many bags. And it makes getting in and out of that very easy. After you've been camping a few times, this will be even clearer because the quicker you can put your hands on what you need to cook or what have you, the better off you are.

COMPILING BOXES

If you don't have any boxes and you're starting from scratch you want to think about your physical capabilities.

SKILLS FOR CAMPING

Say you have a bad back or you're not very strong, then don't buy giant containers and stuff them full of things. Instead, buy small boxes.

If you're putting them in the bed of a pickup then you can have bigger boxes and get away with it. If you're transporting them in the trunk of your car, smaller boxes that are packed more efficiently will definitely help.

DRY-FIT BOXES OR BAGS INTO YOUR TRUNK

If you are purchasing boxes, take everything out of your trunk and test-fit them to make sure they fit properly. Or measure the boxes and return to your trunk to make sure they'll fit before you purchase them. Remember it may have to go in at an angle and turn as often trunk openings are fairly small.

Boxes unloaded and ready to setup camp kitchen

You can also utilize plastic or reusable grocery bags as they're soft and you can stuff them in places. Another option is canvas tote bags; they are more firm but can be squished into smaller spots.

WHAT NEEDS TO BE KEPT DRY?

For example, our kitchen boxes can all sit out in the

rain. We usually pull them under a shelter if there is space, but if they get wet it doesn't matter. Hard plastic, waterproof containers are nice. On the other hand, your sleeping bag needs to stay dry. So, plan out where items will be transported in your car for unpacking purposes.

BE COMFORTABLE DRIVING TO THE CAMPSITE

If your family is like ours, they may be packed into the car like sardines. That is when proper packing techniques make the trip comfortable. When there is room to spread out and relax on the car ride, your weekend starts out on a positive note. Soft-sided bags around the backseat area instead of hard boxes make for a more satisfying traveling space.

START OUT SIMPLE AND INEXPENSIVE

You don't need expensive boxes to camp. If you don't have any containers, purchase inexpensive ones to start so that you can test out your approach when you're camping. If need be you can circle back around and figure out what worked and what didn't. Say you bought a ten dollar container from Home Depot that didn't work, feel free to use it elsewhere in the house. But if you had purchased a three-hundred-dollar aluminum box that doesn't fit where you expected it to, then you're out three hundred bucks. If you find you are camping frequently, you can always replace your supplies with nicer ones.

USE SPACE EFFECTIVELY

When you use your space effectively, you may find you don't need the trailer you've been lugging behind you, or the rooftop cargo carrier. Pack all your kitchen stuff together. All clothing goes in one bag or box, all bedding in another. Your fire building supplies will be grouped as one. All this helps when you arrive at your campsite.

Make sure things that will be left out are in waterproof containers. Pack like things together so that you can put your hands on what you need quickly. And, enjoy your weekend!

SEVEN

WATER FOR DRINKING

Water is something we take for granted every day. When you turn on the faucet, water comes out. Bottled water and fruit drinks sit in the refrigerator. You use water on a daily basis—flushing the toilet, taking a shower, washing dishes, and doing laundry to name a few.

Remember the rules of three we talked about earlier—you can live for three minutes without oxygen, three days without water, and three weeks without food. Our goal in this chapter is discussing safe and clean water for your various activities.

DIFFERENT TYPES OF WATER

When we go camping, we need two different types of water. One is water we're confident is potable (or drinkable). So, when you see potable water, you can drink it. Another is water that's safe to use for cooking, washing and so forth.

POTABLE WATER

If water isn't potable, you should not drink it. Once water is boiled, it is possibly potable. Boiling probably won't remove chemicals or other contaminants in the water, though it may kill the bacteria. Boiled water can still contain unhealthy chemicals and solids.

One source of clean water is sealed bottles. Even though they are a hundred times more expensive than getting it out of the tap, when camping there usually isn't a place that dispenses clean water. Plastic bottles are easy. We always bring single-serve bottles of water as well as gallon jugs, or refillable three to seven gallon jugs, of water. The refillable jugs are commonly blue in color and available at sporting goods stores for less than fifteen dollars each.

When I bring refillable jugs of water, I always clean the jug at home and then fill it with tap water before we leave. That way I know I'm confident I have a source of potable water. I also add a small amount of Clorox when refilling the jug at home.

Make sure you don't leave soap in the jugs when you clean them because if you ingest soap you can get an upset stomach.

I find single-serve water bottles are easiest to handle while camping and hiking as they are potable.

RESEARCH FOR YOURSELF

You probably want to research to understand what potable water is and what is not. I'm going to tell you right now you should never drink out of an open water source like a creek or a lake. Those sources are likely to be contaminated. Let's face it, a hundred years ago, our ancestors who were outside a lot more and didn't have the water supply we have, they probably had immunities to some of these things. You want to make sure you protect your water source and obtain water from a source you trust. Trusted water is either sealed bottles or water you drew from your tap at home.

HOW TO MAKE UNCLEAN WATER POTABLE

If you want to drink out of a creek, you need to filter that water, or you need to chemically treat it. I have a Katadyn filter for when we go backpacking. I take it as a backup source of water. That way, if I run out of water I can filter out of a creek. Boiling water and using a filter has limitations––some things don't filter out because they are too small. So, it's important to have an understanding of how the treatments work.

There are chemical tablets you can put in unclean water; they're easy. But those have a waiting period, twenty to thirty minutes. You've also need to be careful that you never get unclean water in the threads of your container, because the chemical treatment isn't going to reach there. No matter which way you decide to treat or filter the water, there are a lot of things you've got to be on the lookout for.

There are locations where viruses are common, so that knowledge may impact your choice of water treatment. Given these concerns, I would suggest bringing your own water, and then you don't have the hassle. You can catch some really nasty diseases from drinking unclean water.

FILL REUSABLE WATER BOTTLES WITH GALLON JUGS

Refillable 3-5 gallon containers are great for camping

There are inexpensive water containers, I use the ones from Nalgene for personal drinking use. They seem to last forever and hold about a quart.

If you're looking for a five or seven gallon jug for potable or non-potable water, Reliance makes a jug with a spout. If you fill up your own water container, think through contamination points. Make sure your hands are clean before you handle any of the components. Make sure the container is clean and no residual soap is left behind. Adding a tablespoon of

Clorox helps keep the water in the refillable jug safe to drink.

PROTECT WATER FROM CONTAMINATION

When you arrive at your campsite, you need to protect your water from getting contaminated. If there's a lid, be careful about leaving it off for too long. Always make sure your hands are clean before dealing with potable water.

If the jug has a spigot for cleaning hands, make sure you don't touch it with dirty hands or you'll contaminate it. Sometimes a partner makes that even easier to rinse the water.

HAND SANITIZER WARNING

Consider bypassing hand sanitizer as it only cleans the outer layer of germs on your hands. Soap lifts debris, dirt, and contaminants away from your skin and washes away under water.

Instead of using the alcohol-based stuff, actually bring soap and wash your hands with soap and water.

Hand sanitizer can also be used as a fire starter.

WHEN COOKING

Make sure to wash your hands first. I totally agree that if you're cooking outside, leaves and dust will land in your food, but that won't hurt you. What can make you sick is if you have feces from where you didn't wash your hands good after going to the bathroom. Just a tiny amount can make you very, very sick. Most of the time, you've got to guard against the stuff you brought in your body.

THINK AHEAD ABOUT POSSIBLE WATER SOURCES

You'll either bring all the water you'll need, or you'll purchase it somewhere like a grocery store as your trip progresses. A lot of commercial campsites (or state-run sites) have faucets and spigots where you can obtain clean, potable water. You still may want to have some water for on-the-go and you will need a container to put potable water in from the campsite. So, consider investing in a couple of ten dollar jugs.

LIGHTWEIGHT TRAILER

When you're traveling with a lightweight trailer, the water jugs are also a great way to add some weight to the front of the trailer, which helps it tow better. So, you kind of get two uses out of that.

Now, having said that, if you empty your water jug while you're camping, then on your way back, you need to make sure the trailer is not going to blow out. You can either tie it in place or fill it back up with water from a spigot at the campsite, assuming you have one. That way you've got the jugs weighted back down.

HYGIENE

At home, you have running water, both hot and cold, and ample soap and towels to wash hands. Hygiene is much easier at home versus camping. It's something you need to keep in the back of your mind as you carry out tasks at the campsite.

If you can keep yourself healthy while you're camping, then you're definitely going to have a better experience. Keep your hands clean, wash your dishes, and don't leave soap on the dishes or pans.

Some campsites have showers available, use them. If there are no showers, bring ample water so you can clean yourself thoroughly on a daily basis.

HOW MUCH WATER TO BRING

As a rule of thumb, when you're in your home, the average person uses three-to-five gallons of water per day for basic activities like showering, cooking, washing hands, shaving, going to the bathroom. And depending on your toilet and showerhead, you can use a lot more than that.

When camping, you'll probably be more conscious about your water usage. You may not shower or shave, and there may not be toilets to flush. So, I'd guess in the camping arena, each person would use about a gallon a day. If you have a family of five, that calculates to five gallons a day. If you're gone two days, you'll need ten gallons, which is a lot. Maybe you can skate by with six or seven.

If the campsite provides water that makes it easy, if they don't, you need to bring water with you. Trust me; it's better to have excess water than not enough. Water is inexpensive.

There are places out west where water is very difficult to find, so your whole trip may be planned around obtaining water, especially on a longer trip.

DRINKING WATER

Keep in mind if you're in the southwest of the U.S., or even in Texas or Colorado, where it's not very humid, the amount of water your body consumes is much higher because it's used for sweating and cooling your body off in perspiration. Therefore, you may go through twice as much water in New Mexico or Colorado than in North Carolina, because North Carolina has high humidity and water doesn't evaporate as quickly.

At the same time, if it's in the summer, you're going to use more water because it's hot outside and you need to stay well hydrated. Make sure everybody's drinking the water they need because the best place for water is inside your body, not in the jug.

Also, remember that if you consume a lot of water at home, you're going to consume a lot camping.

WHAT DOES "PRIMITIVE CAMPSITE" MEAN?

There is no water, no toilet facilities, and obviously no shower accommodations.

If the information says primitive plus toilet facilities, then it will be real simple—a box above a hole in the ground, type of thing.

More of a full-service campground will state what amenities are available. Any amenities (i.e., showers, bathrooms, water spigots) that aren't listed, you should assume they're not available. Bring a few extra gallons of water. If you don't use it, you're not out much; but you've got some peace of mind and you've been prepared. That way you don't have some horrible surprise that puts you driving back to town just to track down water, which could be a long way depending on your location.

WRAP UP

Keep everybody well hydrated. Use good hygiene. Have clean water. Remember the Rule of Three from earlier? Well this chapter covered number two, hydration.

When you first start camping, keep it real simple. Don't travel too far away from home so you can enjoy your trip. If you consume a lot of water at home, you're going to consume a lot of water while you are camping. As long as you have access to water, or bring enough water with you, then you are okay. Trying to suddenly change your

SKILLS FOR CAMPING

family's water habits just adds stress, however you may be able to create a teachable moment where you emphasis conservation. By planning ahead, you plan for the worst and enjoy the success of being prepared.

EIGHT

SHOWERS AND CAMP HYGIENE

When you're camping, there are a few different options on the shower scene. If you're going to be gone overnight, you may not intend on taking a shower, especially if you're not exerting yourself and sweating. You may plan to shower at home before you leave and then again when you return home. If you're going to be gone the whole weekend or longer then showering becomes a bigger issue. Hygiene's always important, and it's always good to be prepared with a way to shower, or at least wash off, if you get dirty. You may slip and fall in the mud, or a child gets filthy, so it's always good to have a towel or some way of cleaning off, even if it's only partially. On longer trips, it becomes a bigger issue.

Hygiene is important. Brushing your teeth every morning is good for relations with other people. Washing your face in the morning and in the evening can be done without running water as well. Don't forget to wash your hands before eating or cooking to prevent dysentery.

SOME CAMPSITES HAVE SHOWER FACILITIES

This is nice because all you need is a towel, a washcloth, soap, and flip-flops. Public showers tend to stay wet, which opens you up to catch athlete's foot or toenail fungus. I'm not a medical person but I can tell you that flip-flops are a good way to prevent this issue. Bring them for everyone using a communal shower. It's also nice, too, after you take a shower; you may not want to put your shoes back on immediately. You may want to let your feet kind of air out a little bit, especially if it's been raining over the weekend or you've been active all day. I've gotten to where, when I go camping, I shower just about every night.

Typical shower at a campground

WHERE YOU'RE CAMPING DOESN'T HAVE A SHOWER FACILITY

Without a shower facility, you have two scenarios. One is that you have a lot of people around you and you don't have an opportunity to take a shower easily because there's no privacy. In that case there are a couple options.

A pop up cabana is a great way to have privacy for a shower or other uses

One is a pop-up cabana or shelter, they're about three by three at the bottom and seven feet tall. Usually you stake them down and they pop up. Some of them have poles you slide in like a tent. Others are this pop-up design where you turn them loose and you pull in one direction and they kind of snap in place. Those are a great way to have a place with privacy for a shower. Bring a bucket of soapy water, a bucket of rinse water, a washcloth and a towel, and you can achieve a lot of the benefits of having a regular shower. I call it a bucket shower. You can accomplish a pretty decent bath this way. These cabanas or shelters are inexpensive. They are also multi-use because you can change in them. You can use them for years because they'll spend a couple days outdoors a few times a year. They are also handy in other places where you need some privacy.

Another possibility is to put up a shower. This is what we do when we go camping at our place. I have a deer cleaning stand which doubles as a shower holder. We take a solar bag for heating water, called a solar shower. They work surprisingly well in warm weather. You lay the full bag out in the sun all day and by evening the water's warm enough so you're not going to shiver when the water hits you. You hang the bag up in the air above the shower. Your goal is to get wet, turn the water off, soap up your body, then turn the water back on and rinse. If you minimize your water usage, there's a really good chance you can probably shower in a gallon and a half of water. If you've got long hair to wash, that will take more water. A gallon and a half is about how much water you need for each person in the family, for each shower. You'll need a solar bag for each person showering every day. Fill them up with water, lay them out in the sun during the day and let them warm up. I will caution you not to lay the bag on the ground, as the ground is probably cooler than the surrounding air during the day, so the bag won't heat up as much. Lay the solar bag up off the ground, say on the table, or a chair, or a bench, to get warmer. These solar bags are inexpensive, about eight to fifteen dollars. In my mind it's a disposable item. After some number of times of use, the bag will die because it isn't expensive plastic. So, it's probably a good idea to have an extra one, just in case.

If you don't have trees in the right spot to hang the bag from, the solar shower can be a little problematic so you may

Solar showers can work great

need to get creative. One possibility is to use the back of your vehicle. You can always set the solar bag on top of your SUV, using your SUV as an anchor point. Then simply have two people hold up a shower curtain. With some creativity, you can come up with a way to give everyone a few minutes' worth of privacy to shower.

If you want hot water you can always heat some water over the fire, and then mix in some cold water to where it's comfortable to use in your solar shower. If the sun didn't heat up your solar shower then you can always take a funnel and fill it with warm water from the fire and then hang it up. Another way to make a shower stall is to take a tarp or some sort of a nylon fly and string it between some trees with some Paracord or some twine or rope. Always check the water temperature to make sure it isn't too hot to spray on your body.

SEMI-PERMANENT STAND FOR A POP-UP SHOWER

On our property in western North Carolina, I actually have a two-foot by two foot deck that's made of plastic and salt-treated boards. When we leave the property, we stand it up so when it rains, the rain washes the dirt off. When we use the shower, we just lay the deck flat and have a fairly somewhat clean place to stand. We do use flip-flops for the shower and walk back down to camp where we put on our shoes. We have also used this in a popup

SKILLS FOR CAMPING

cabana. Something like this could easily be transported with your gear.

ORGANIZATION IS THE KEY

Know where you're going and what's available. Do you have to bring some sort of cabana to make a shower, or do you have an opportunity to hang up a solar shower? Or maybe there is a shower on-site.

I love to take a long shower at the end of the day. It's relaxing and a good way to end the day before you start cooking dinner or while dinner's being cooked. It definitely makes the camping experience feel less grimy. You kids may even look back on the trip with a different opinion because of a shower. If they got to go to bed clean and woke up clean, they'll be more apt to want to go camping again! Because of this, I would encourage you to find a shower strategy because I really think it changes everyone's outlook.

Everyone having a personal hygiene kit keeps things moving in the morning

SEGREGATE WATER

If you go to a place you've never been before, take your own water. Bring bottled water to drink from. Or water in a container. One strategy is to use local, potable water from a faucet or other safe source for things like showering and washing dishes. Then use bottled water for drinking. This way you don't run the risk of introducing a family member to water with different mineral content that might upset a sensitive stomach. Brush your teeth and drink from that drinking water. If you're going to make Kool-Aid, you use the water you brought. You can cook, wash dishes, and shower with the local water. You do need to be careful with kids, as they may not be as careful about ingesting water when they shower. Consider potable water for their showers.

HOW MUCH WATER DO YOU NEED?

You're probably going to consume roughly three to five gallons per person per day in a non-arid environment. If you're in an arid climate, like a desert or in the Southwest, then you may consume six or seven gallons a day. It's important to think about how much water you're going to need. If you're at a campsite with a spigot, you're fine, otherwise you need to bring all your drinking water. Make sure to have plenty of water to keep everybody hydrated. If people become dehydrated they're going to get headaches, they're going to feel bad and it can be dangerous. Of course, if you're in a spot that's more arid, or you're going to be vigorous with hiking or exercising, then you may also want to consider providing a source of electrolytes like Gatorade or Propel, just to make sure you're not sweating out things you need and not replacing them in your food and drink.

BATHROOMS

If you're at a campground, they're going to provide bathrooms. If you are at a more primitive location, where they don't have a restroom, you'll have to create your own bathroom. You can urinate in the woods somewhere private. If you're a woman you can go in the woods, too. Women do it every day across American forests, so it's not a big deal. If you have someone who absolutely can't urinate without sitting down, then use a bucket specially set aside for urination. It's more to manage but that's a good concession. In some arid locations, there may be limits on free range urinating. In those spots, there are usually outdoor bathrooms near areas where you would stop to camp.

For defecation I recommend a three or five gallon bucket, with a camping snap-on toilet seat. You'll need to purchase either paper shredder bags from an office store or disposable waste bags from a camping store specifically made for this purpose. Use the liner for the bucket, and then snap on the toilet seat lid. When a liner has been used, tie it up and then put it in another liner, keeping the defecation bags away from the campsite for odor reasons. Every time a liner is used, add it to a larger and thicker trash bag that you hang from a tree. The beauty of these things is they really don't become dirty. You simply wipe off the toilet seat and the bucket has a liner in it. I would highly recommend using a specific bucket for this one purpose. You can mark it with a Sharpie.

Now I will warn you not to urinate in this special bucket because extra liquids will make it harder to transport. The goal is to have the baggies only contain defecation.

Be very careful because you have defecation in a bucket when you transport your trash and waste. If that spills or the bag tears you will have defecation in your car. A buddy of mine did this. Instead of keeping all the liners tied and placed in a larger bag, he just threw them in the back of his truck thinking he'd dispose of them when he got down the mountain. Except, when he got to the bottom of the mountain, some stuff in the truck shifted and there was poop all over the back of his vehicle.

Toilet in a bucket works great

You can set up this portable toilet in your cabana to make it dual use. A lot of the cabanas don't have floors. If you get a mess on the ground under the bottom of the cabana, simply move it to a new location. Those waste bags work really well. There's really no smell. The first time you can dispose of the bag, do so because then you're less likely to have a mess.

Those lids are very inexpensive; they're just a few dollars. You can purchase the buckets at a hardware or home improvement store for about three bucks each. It doesn't really matter if the bucket is food grade or not. I have a bucket with a toilet seat on it, and we carried that for a long time to the top of the mountain where we go camping. Then a friend bought me a porta potty to put on top of the mountain. What a great gift. It's easy to keep clean. We have a service come and empty it a couple times a year. It's an amazingly nice convenience. If you want a porta-potty for land you have, buy a used one. They are much cheaper and there really isn't much difference from a new one after a few months. Of course, you can't take a porta-potty with you; it's more of a permanent thing. But that bucket with the snap on toilet seat works well and is portable.

LEAVE NO TRACE

If you have to poop on the trail or outside, always bury the poop and the toilet paper. Keeping a small shovel or a sturdy kitty litter scoop with you is really helpful. Don't leave used toilet paper or defecation out in the open. That is horrible to walk up on and see. It spoils the experience for someone who comes behind you.

WRAP UP

Hopefully these ideas will help you organize your campsite with respect to hygiene, bathing, urination, and defecation. Most of these things we discussed were not very expensive. Some of them were multiple use items as well.

NINE

PITCH YOUR TENT

Before we delve into the technical part of how and where to pitch your tent, let me tell you a story. About fifteen years ago, when my kids were younger, I went camping with my two daughters. We had purchased a new giant tent from Sears and Roebuck. At the time, Hurricane Bob was somewhere in the Georgia-South Carolina area as we headed out of North Carolina to the Shenandoah National Forest. The forecasters weren't sure what was going to happen, but the storm was close to getting downgraded so we decided to go camping based on that news. I told my girls that if the weather got really bad, we could drive to a hotel fifteen minutes away and climb into warm beds.

Needless to say, we set up camp and the rain started. I mean, poured. We rode out that hurricane, which was downgraded to a tropical storm, in a tent in the Shenandoah National Forest. It rained for twenty-four hours. I will tell you that rain, when you are sitting in a house, is completely different than rain when you are in a tent. That weekend, we read a lot, had deep discussions, and enjoyed a memorable time. The only negative event was during the night the tent leaked. We woke up and our air mattress was floating in a foot of water. Thankfully we had planned ahead and all of our belongings were in waterproof containers. I bet my girls will never forget Hurricane Bob in a tent. My point for you is to always be prepared; I don't discuss waterproof boxes for nothing!

WHY THE NEED FOR PLANNING?

Your tents well-being is critical because if it rains, it keeps you dry. Staying dry and being out of the elements also make people feel more comfortable and warm. It's a clean area where you can kind of get away from the outdoors. There's also a psychological benefit when you go into a tent, you've got a sleeping bag, you've got your dry clothes, and you are able to keep your stuff organized. That is why a sturdy and leak proof tent is so valuable to you.

The goal is to climb into your tent and feel like you're in a home away from home. That way, your family will sleep well, they'll have a great time, and they'll want to go back.

MAKE SURE YOU HAVE ALL THE STAKES AND POLES BEFORE YOU LEAVE HOME

Before you take a tent camping, make sure you have enough stakes and poles. I recommend putting it up in the back yard before you go. If you arrive at the campsite to discover you are missing a pole, there's no good way to overcome that. Yeah you might use a stick from a tree in a pinch, but it could tear the fabric or the stick could break and the tent may fall down in the middle of the night— not a winning situation on your first camping trip. Your tent is an important piece. Setting up the tent before you go is just as important for a new or used one.

IF YOU BORROW A TENT

If you borrow a tent, I recommend putting it up before you go camping to inspect the livability. Look for tears and places of wear as well as other things that would cause problems or leaks. If the fabric looks like something's worn to the point it might cause a leak, then don't take a chance, use a different tent.

Check for mildew. If you open the tent and smell mildew or see black spots, you should really question whether or not you want to take it. Every time we've seen tents with mildew, they ended up leaking. Something about mildew attacks the waterproofing. Usually once a tent starts mildewing it becomes less reliable. You don't want a tent to fail in a rainstorm, because that will ruin the trip.

BE PREPARED, RAIN IS ALWAYS A POSSIBILITY

The reality is you'll probably get some rain if you're in the Appalachian Mountains at some point over the weekend. Other places, like the western part of the country in the high desert for example, would be much less likely to see rain. But you might; you never know. It really depends on where you are camping. Always check the weather forecast, be prepared for rain and other unexpected weather.

PREVAILING WINDS

Figure out which direction the prevailing winds are coming from. If the weather is warm, plan to have the wind run down the length of the tent to cool the inside. If it's cold outside, you probably want to turn the tent so the wind is blocked. It's a minor thing but might make a few degrees of difference. If the weather is frigid, you don't want a prevailing wind going in a direction where it can get underneath the rainfly and cool off the tent. Generally, wind goes across a ridge, not along the ridge. Spend a few minutes and notice the wind. When the wind direction changes, it often comes from the opposite direction. When you pitch your tent, keep this in mind.

If you have a ten-by-twenty tent like we do, and it's

windy, you probably want the long axis, or the smallest face of the tent facing the oncoming wind. That way the wind can generate less force against the tent. If you turn the tent so the wind is constantly blowing at the largest face, you've created a giant sail which will be harder on your equipment.

CHECK FOR DRAINAGE

Check the ground to verify rainwater will flow away from your tent. If a heavy rain begins, where will the water drain? If you're out west and see sand in the middle of a dry riverbed, don't pitch your tent there because you may wake up in a huge mess. Instead make sure your tent isn't sitting where water normally flows during a rain. The goal is for your tent to not flood because it can be dangerous as the tent and all the contents can get swept away. Or the water can build up in your tent, which makes a mess.

Suffice it to say, pitch your tent on high ground. At the same time, you may not want to be at the top of a super windy mountain. If I had to choose between windy or rain-deluged, I'd rather be in a windy spot because getting caught in a flash flood can be deadly. The best case is to find a spot where your tent is protected from the wind and any potential water flows. If you are in a campsite, then you will have a designated place to pitch your tent.

You'll see in some older books people would dig a channel around their tent. If you have to dig a ditch around your tent to keep water away, then you're pitching your tent in the wrong spot. If everyone puts a channel around their tent, the ground takes on a tremendous amount of damage. It is considered vandalism and you could be kicked out of the campground or receive a ticket. Leave no trace when you camp. Your goal should always be to leave the campsite in a better condition than when you arrived.

CHOOSE A SPOT PROTECTED FROM WEATHER

If you can keep a hill or a mountain between you and the prevailing wind, you end up with a little more pleasant camping experience just because you're not feeling the full force of gusty winds. Also, if you're on the backside of the mountain you may not get hit with as much rain. So there again it's worthwhile looking around to see where water has been. If there's been a lot of water flowing there, it's definitely not the place you want for your tent.

SURVEY THE GROUND

Before you put your tent down, look for protrusions like rocks and saplings or things that stick up from the ground that can either tear the tent floor or make it miserable to sleep on. You also want to think about how hard the ground is. If possible, find a grassy knoll to sleep on that's smooth and comfortable.

Normally your feet are lower than your head when

you sleep. So, orient your sleeping bag and tent so that when you crawl in, your feet are downhill. That will make a lot more comfortable camping experience. If you pitch your tent where there is a steep incline, you can develop a headache while sleeping.

USE A "FOOTPRINT" OR A TARP

A footprint is typically a nylon piece that generally snaps onto the bottom of the tent. If you purchase a tent and a footprint's available, always buy it. The footprint gives you an extra layer between the tent and the ground, and helps prevent damage to the bottom of the tent. It also helps keep bugs and water out, and helps your tent last longer.

In lieu of a footprint, you can use a tarp. We do that a lot with our big tent. We have this gigantic, palatial tent that is wonderful because there's tons of room. To keep it waterproof, we layer a tarp underneath and then fold the edges of the tarp where it sticks out underneath the tarp and underneath the

The foot print (to the right) protects the bottom of the tent

tent. This helps prevent water from seeping up from the ground into the tent, and also protects the tent floor like a footprint would. It's kind of a poor man's footprint. By the way, having an extra tarp is handy in case something goes sideways.

PITCH YOUR TENT

You have selected the location, now you need to pitch your tent. The steps are very similar for most modern tents as they are self-supporting. For example if you take a dome tent and put it together, the dome tent will support the walls and the roof without being staked to the ground. Staking it to the ground locates it and also pulls the panels tight and keeps them from getting blown away.

When you put up a tent, you're going to have poles that you slide in or that snap in place. Some of the big tents will have structures that snap together. They are usually called easy-up or quick-assembly tents. Once the poles are in place, your tent is self-supporting.

INSTALL THE FLY

Next you put the fly over the tent. Not all tents have a fly but most do. The fly creates a space between the top of the tent and the weather. Depending on the construction of the tent, it may be that your tent actually has mesh on the top. The fly sits on top of the poles and keeps rain from coming through the mesh. A cabin style tent may only have one layer. The mesh is nice in warm weather because it lets air flow underneath.

Usually the rain fly will snap or tie to some sort of piece at the base of the pole, then pull the bottom tight. I would suggest starting with one corner, stake that down; and then pull it taut on the next corner and work your way around. Don't put all the stakes in at once, start with the corner stakes and stretch the fabric pieces taut without many big wrinkles in them. The fabric fly material should not be hanging down to where it's touching the side wall of the top ceiling of the tent. The pressure can tend to spread the fibers and make them leak. It truly depends on the fabric you are using, but it's in your best interest to get this tent put up nice and tight. And then go back and add all the other stakes.

Make sure the panels are taut

There are corner stakes, stakes between the corner stakes, and stakes for the flies. In some areas you'll need a hammer because soil is extremely hard. If you don't have a hammer, you can use a rock. A hammer's something you probably have in your toolbox anyways, so bring it with you. The hammer can also be handy for removing the stakes as sometimes they are hard to remove. You don't want to pull on the body of the tent to pull the stakes out because you can rip the tent. Instead, you can take your hammer and just pull them right out.

WORKAROUND, PLACE A TARP OVER A LEAKING TENT

In a bind you can put a tarp over your tent. That's a solution when you don't have another option. The tent is a complex piece of sewn fabric and a tarp is not. There will be areas that will probably get wet, even if you try to cover it as best you can. That's a way to mitigate the amount of water that gets in, but may not stop it completely. I've seen people put a tarp over the tent and they'll put poles or hang it from a tree so the tarp is actually suspended above the tent. A tent that needs a tarp above it to keep from leaking probably needs to be replaced or repaired. A non-functional tent isn't the one you want for your first camping trip.

HANDY TIP

Another good thing to carry is a few extra tent stakes, because even if you don't use them there's a really good chance you have a buddy who will need them. Also, don't forget a hammer for installing and removing stakes. In fact, bringing a toolbox is never a bad idea.

WHEN YOU COME HOME, DRY OUT YOUR TENT

Once you arrive home put your tent somewhere to

dry. If it's bone dry outside when you put up and took down your tent, then maybe it can go in the bag. Be careful, though, because the bottom of the tent might be damp. Moisture can become trapped in a folded up tent and cause mildew, which will cause you problems down the road. When I get back home I lay the tent out on the garage floor, making sure all the folds of plastic fabric can air dry. By doing this, your tent will last longer.

SUMMARY FOR SELECTING A CAMPSITE

Don't forget to check out your tent before you leave home. Even if you bought it brand-new, put it up. That way you know how to put it up and you make sure you have everything necessary. Your tent site should be free from water runoff so you can remain safe and dry. Consider the prevailing wind and whether you want to use it as air conditioning or a buffer during cooler temperatures.

I've pitched a lot of tents and had very few failures. My failures were lack of preparation ahead of time. I will also say I've had a new tent fail, though it was inexpensive. We rode out Hurricane Bob in that thing and it leaked like a sieve. I take care of tents. My two-man tent, an REI quarter dome, I've carried that thing all over. I've slept in it for years. It started leaking in a few places. So when my stepson kept borrowing it, I finally just gave it to him. I need to replace that tent with another half-dome because

SKILLS FOR CAMPING

I got fifteen years of multiple camping trips a year out of the first one.

Finally, when you pack up your tent for storage, make sure everything is in the bag. I'm embarrassed to say that I was in a remote spot quickly putting up my tent on the top of a mountain. And as rain began to fall, I realized my rain fly was two-hundred-fifty miles away in Raleigh! I used a spare tarp to cover the tent. It was an okay solution that kept me mostly dry, but much better than sleeping in the rain. Without that tarp, it would have been a very difficult weekend. I now make sure to double check that everything is in my tent bag when I pack it up for storage. And I always bring an extra tarp.

Typical campsite in a campground

TEN

CAMP KITCHEN

Your camp kitchen is where you organize all your food, utensils, pots, and pans. Depending on the amount of cooking you plan, that will drive how much of a camp kitchen you will need. For example, if you're camping overnight and plan on eating sandwiches for dinner and bagels for breakfast, organization is simple. Once you start cooking over the fire and have multiple days as well as multiple meals, then staying organized helps keep you focused on enjoying the trip, not looking for an item that you can't find.

SEPARATING EQUIPMENT INTO LIKE CONTAINERS

We talked about boxes and packing in an earlier chapter. To sum it up, pack like items together. For example, don't bundle cooking utensils with your boots. Store like equipment together so that when you arrive

SKILLS FOR CAMPING

at the campsite you will be able to locate everything. A container for jackets and footwear, one for building a fire, one for food, one for kitchen utensils, one for pots and pans. You get the idea. Containers should be sized to the need and should nest within each other. Boxes within boxes.

Organization allows for you to put your hands on what you're looking for quickly, instead of digging through multiple boxes. This also helps you keep your food, equipment, and supplies clean.

CAMP KITCHEN CONTAINERS

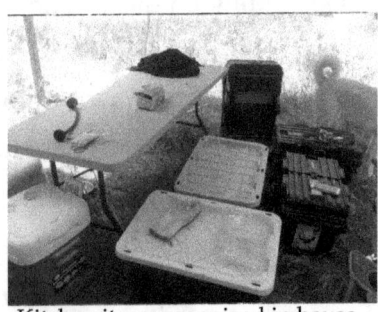
Kitchen items organized in boxes - ready to setup kitchen under shelter and on folding table

I'll tell you how we pack, and you can figure out what works for you. We have food in one box, pots and pans in another, and kitchen supplies in yet another. Of course, cold food is in the cooler.

The three container approach makes it quicker and easier to find what you need. If one big container holds everything, everyone in the campsite will end up digging though the box countless times per day for different items. Keeping one big box organized is very difficult. Using multiple boxes and labeling them helps keep your kitchen organized and makes everything simpler.

One container holds food. For example, prepackaged oatmeal, snacks, fruit, canned goods, bread, ketchup, mustard, salt, pepper, and individual packets of condiments all go in this container. These items are generally only needed at meal time so you want to separate them from non-food supplies that you may need throughout the day.

Keep food separate - helps with staying organized

The second container is kitchen supplies. This includes dry sundries like forks, knives, can opener, matches, paper towels, plastic ware, trash bags, plates, and cups. This is the box you will frequently open so you want to put the most effort into keeping this container organized. A container with built in compartments will give you easy ways to arrange these items. If not, use the "boxes within a box" approach to organize. To identify the content, put labels on small containers for quick access.

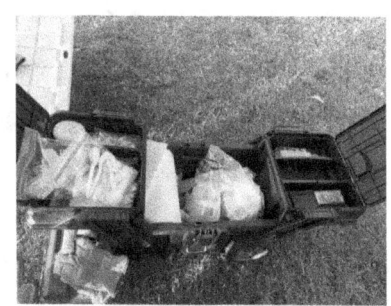
Organized for quick access to sundries

SKILLS FOR CAMPING

The final container is pots and pans. The reason I suggest separating cookware is that at the end of the night, even after you've washed them, there is often still a smoky residue from the bottom of the pot where it sat over the fire. Putting it in with clean items can make a mess. The best solution is to have a separate container for cookware. Also, you usually only need pots and pans at meals, so keep them separated from items needed on a more frequent basis, like paper towels and snacks.

Now, you probably don't want to use your nice pots and pans for camping. If you have an old set, use them. Otherwise you can go to Goodwill for used cookware. You can find aluminum and stainless steel, thin pots. Make sure to snag a frying pan. Later on, you can give this cookware to your kids when they move out of the house for their first apartment.

When you're carrying the pots and pans from your car to the camp kitchen and its twenty feet, something from Goodwill works great, you don't need to invest in ultra-lightweight titanium backpacking pots. There's nothing wrong with going to REI to grab this awesome gear, but if it's your first trip, I'd say figure out if you enjoy camping before you spend gobs of money. You can always upgrade your gear; downgrading is a little harder, because the money's already spent.

ORGANIZATION MAKES IT EASIER TO FIND THINGS

Easily finding things when camping is something you want to focus on because if your stuff is well-organized, you won't have to dig. If you keep your belongings organized and clean, they will be easy to find and then you're back to having fun.

DESIGNATE A POINT PERSON

Often, it's good to have one individual who's managing where everything is located at the campsite. Everybody needs to pitch in, but one person lays everything out and is in charge. That's usually the neat one in the family. Let them take over this task as they'll feel better about it and they'll be more relaxed because everything is in order. You'll benefit from the organization because your life will be a lot easier.

GATHERING TOGETHER ITEMS FOR YOUR CAMP KITCHEN

You may not need to purchase kitchen items for your first trip but here are some things you can use other times, so you may want to invest in them.

The first is a pop-up type shelter which keeps out the sun and some of the rain. These shelters run from fifty to two hundred bucks. You can purchase them at sporting goods stores. A good size would be nine-by-nine or ten-by-ten. They pop up, though it's easier with two people to put them up. They've got a frame and a cover which delineates where your kitchen is, so people aren't running through it.

This shelter can be used at places other than the camp site. We've found it is great to put up beside the grill so you can have a shaded chair when you're cooking. You can also bring it with you to soccer games.

I have found these shelters get beat up, so we tend to purchase the fifty dollar ones. We use them for a few years until they fall apart and then buy another one. We consider these shelters a consumable product. I've tried the Easy-ups, but they are heavier and harder to deal with and take up more space. They do last longer, but we prefer the trade offs of being more portable and easier to set up and tear down.

Organized is happy

The second is a folding table. You can buy a plastic six or eight foot folding table with metal legs for about fifty dollars. The nice thing is you can use it for other tasks at home—maybe a barbecue or crafts or extra people for dinner. You'll want the table with a plastic top because rain will bead off. Tables with wood tops won't do as well with the rain and are heavier to maneuver.

The third is a set of boxes or canvas bags for your dry

goods, a box or canvas bag for delicate groceries, and a container for pots and pans.

SETTING UP THE CAMP KITCHEN

Set up your shelter and place the folding table underneath. Many times I tuck the cooler in there as well to keep it out of the sun, which helps the ice last longer. On that note, leave the water in your cooler as the ice melts to keep the contents cold. The water acts as a thermal mass and so throwing away the water means your ice probably won't last as long.

Then place the items you'll need for the following day on the table. Maybe have a corner of the table reserved for things you use on a regular basis (like salt and pepper, the lighter for the fire, your car keys so everyone knows where they are, your phone so it isn't baking in the sun). Set out your knives and cutting board. Perhaps set out easy-to-grab snacks like apples or individual size chips or energy bars. The point is to organize this area with anything you're going to use again and again.

Hang up trash bag to keep small critters out

The other thing you can do is buy inexpensive tablecloths. We have a tablecloth with felt on one side and plastic on the other that I figured would last one trip, but it's going on ten years! So, go figure. It's got a little tear in one corner but it's easy to clean. A tablecloth is easier to clean than the plastic tables.

Set your box or canvas bag for your dry goods, the box or canvas bag for delicate groceries, and the container for pots and pans near the shelter. Now, everything you need for the kitchen is at your finger-tips.

WHAT KIND OF A COOLER SHOULD YOU USE?

When it comes to coolers, keep in mind the less expensive the cooler, the less material goes into it. So, if you're going overnight, it really doesn't matter what cooler you're taking. If you're going for a week or four days and you don't have access to purchase more ice, quality becomes more important. Keeping the cooler lid shut when you're not using it and not opening it when you don't have to is key to keep the ice for as long as possible.

Chill your drinks and things before you put them in the cooler. For example, if you take a whole case of bottled water and throw it in a cooler, it's going to cause some of the ice to melt because the ice will have to work harder to cool the room-temperature water. One trick I have is to freeze some of the waters, they will help keep the cooler colder longer and they are the ones to grab at the beginning of a long hike as they will stay cold longer.

Keep in mind that in certain climates, soft drinks

and bottled water don't need to be refrigerated. It really depends on the weather where you are. If it's thirty degrees at night and eighty-five during the day and you're in the high desert, you probably don't need to refrigerate it. If you're in Eastern North Carolina on the coast and its ninety-five during the day and eighty-nine at night, you'll need to refrigerate it.

There are Yeti-type coolers that are spectacular, but they're expensive. Ask yourself if you can get by on a short trip with a ten dollar cooler. Will you use it for other things? Probably. So, if you go buy a five hundred dollar yeti cooler, did you add stress to your camping trip because of that money spent? It's all a matter of balance, do what works for your family.

We've got three different coolers we use for a variety of activities. We've got a little six-pack cooler we take when travel to a buddy's place to work on his farm, or if we go to the gym and it's going to be a long trip. We've got a bigger square one that fits in the back of the Jeep that we take four wheeling, or if we go on a day trip somewhere say to the beach. We also have a giant white one, a fishing cooler, that holds a hundred and fifty quarts. I will tell you, the big one gets very heavy when you fill it up, so consider that. On the other hand, I put enough ice in there that I can go three days without replenishing.

It really depends on what you're going to need and what your budget is. There are times when a ten dollar cooler will suffice. It might take you another trip to the store during the middle of your trip, but if you're already going by the store then a few dollar's worth of ice is much better than spending four hundred and fifty dollars on Yeti cooler and saving two dollars on ice.

WRAP UP

Keep your camp kitchen organized. By containing all these things in one place, it means when you look for items it only takes seconds rather than minutes, to put your hands on what you're seeking. You'll also find it'll make packing up quicker.

If you enjoy camping, consider investing in containers that are the perfect size for how you camp. And when you arrive home, you store non-perishable goods in those boxes, perhaps cups, plates, napkins, old pots and pans. Next time you go on a trip, you can pull the containers from storage and you're ready to camp again!

My wife, Connie, tends to be the keeper of the kitchen, probably because she's the organized one. Before we leave on a camping trip, she makes a meal plan, prepares the food, and gathers food items together before we pack the car. But, you'll just have to work it out between the two of you. There's no magic formula, no wrong answer. Everybody's different. The trick is to be tender and loving and kind when you're doing it, and not fight over unimportant stuff. That way you can enjoy the camping more.

For now, keep it inexpensive and simple and joyous. As your sense of adventure grows, then maybe one day you'll try true backpacking trips with ninety miles of trail in front of you. I tell you, those are awesome. I enjoy backpacking and the rugged hikes. On the other hand, I've also enjoyed just going down the road to the lake and camping overnight.

Kids grow up quick, so don't wait too long to take them camping. Teach them good skills. Enjoy those priceless memories and build those relationships. Don't skip going for a quick weekend trip because you want to take an epic journey "some day." Some days often don't happen and you're missing the momentous fun you could have on the simple, "non-epic" trip.

Set up and ready for hot dog and hamburger dinner

ELEVEN

FIRST AID

When you go camping, sometimes you're away from civilization and sometimes not. Some campsites, let's call them urban campsites, are pretty close to hospitals and grocery stores. Of course, there are campsites where you're in the middle of nowhere. A good example in North Carolina, if you go to the Jordan Lake campground, you're fifteen minutes from a major hospital. If you go to where we camp on Troublesome Gap, you're an hour-and-a-half from the nearest hospital. In the same state you can see two totally different situations. If you're out West, you might be hours—or in some cases, even days—from help. At Philmont Scout Ranch in New Mexico, there's a good chance it could be twenty-four hours before assistance arrives. Keep in mind that most campsites you go to probably aren't super far from a town or emergency help.

THE CLOSEST HOSPITAL

Knowing the location of the closest hospital is important because it may impact your decision making process. If you're an hour-and-a-half away, calling an ambulance may mean you may not see one for an hour or more. That means you've got to provide trauma and first aid on the victim until help arrives. Optionally you can drive to meet the ambulance or drive the victim to the hospital.

INFORMATION IS KNOWLEDGE

If you choose to camp far from civilization, make sure everybody in your group is aware of where they are and can explain the location so the 911 dispatcher understands. This is critical in the event of an emergency. Don't assume your locale can be triangulated using cell tower information, as that only works well in the movies. Everyone in your group needs to know how to precisely describe your location.

WHAT EXACTLY 9-1-1 NEEDS TO KNOW

You need to make sure everybody in your group can communicate where they are to the dispatcher. For example, when we go camping at our place at Troublesome Gap, there's a street address associated with our property. Because the street address has never had an active mailbox, it's in very few databases. It's in the post office database, but it may not be in the emergency dispatcher database. We found this out when I called ULOCO to locate a power line and they wouldn't do it because they couldn't identify the location of the property.

We teach everybody what to say if they are in an accident and call 9-1-1, state what county you're in, that you're on Baltimore Branch Road, and then add Troublesome Gap. At that point, you need to give the dispatcher an idea of which side of the gap. One easy way is there's a cell tower nearby and everybody in the county knows where it is. So, if you tell them you're up near the cell tower they know where you are.

EVEN KIDS

Make sure everyone in your group is familiar with this information. You never know what could happen. You and your wife could be having a great time and you both bump your heads together and pass out. You're probably laughing right now saying what's the likelihood of that? But when people get stressed out, crazy things happen. For example, let's say you broke your leg and it's a compound fracture and its ugly and your wife passes out. Or, vise versa. When someone calls 9-1-1, they need to know what to say and where to send the ambulance. Some places have Life Flight, or a helicopter, but it's important to understand to call the helicopter only in absolute time-sensitive emergencies, say something that's going to kill you in the next hour if you don't get help. A heart attack would be a good example. Or you've done internal damage to your organs, or you're bleeding out, or you have a gunshot wound. Triage the incident properly. Just because someone's in a lot of pain doesn't mean they've got to ride on a helicopter.

TRIAGE

When something goes wrong, take a look at the situation, figure out the injuries, and take steps to treat it. Break the symptoms down into what's really the risk. If someone's having a heart attack, they need to be on the way to meet the ambulance, or on the way to the hospital when they first realize they are having a heart attack. There's no waiting around, there's no picking up anything, you leave.

If a person is not breathing, make sure someone calls for help while you give first aid. If someone's heart stops beating, then you stay where you are and give them CPR. If it's a broken bone and your child (or your husband) is screaming in pain, that does not mean the 9-1-1 operator will send a Life Flight helicopter to rescue you. If it's a cut with manageable bleeding, the smartest thing to do is drive them to the hospital.

Only if it is significant trauma or injury do you need to call 9-1-1. If it truly is life threatening, the dispatcher will figure out the best way to get you where they can treat you, or bring treatment to you as quickly as possible.

MAKE DECISIONS

Feel free to talk through the symptoms with the dispatcher. They deal with these types of situations every day. If you are not sure what to do in an emergency situation, ask the 9-1-1 operator as they are there to help.

Think through what the best answer is for the situation presenting itself. Should you take the injured party to the hospital in a car? Is it to call an ambulance? If it's a minor injury, there's a pretty good chance the best solution is to hop in the car and drive them to the hospital. If it's a serious injury, then calling an ambulance is smart.

If the ambulance is an hour-and-a-half away, the dispatcher may make provisions for you to meet the ambulance halfway. You have to be cool, calm, and collected to make sure you're getting the best outcome for the injured person.

If you're not emotionally or physically in a state to drive, then don't. Call 9-1-1 and wait on the ambulance.

FIRST RESPONDER

The other thing to keep in mind is the first person to arrive may not be an ambulance, but a firefighter. What happens is you may have a local fire department and they will come and provide first aid. The local fire department has a solid level of first aid training that's not as intense as the paramedics, which is not as intense as the ER.

LEARN FIRST AID SKILLS

Knowledge weighs nothing. If you go and take a first aid and CPR class, you are ahead of the game, because now you have a baseline to start from. You'll operate from this training in an emergency. Anytime you're in a difficult situation, you're going to sink to your most basic level of training. If you've had ten basic first aid classes and one slightly advanced class, you're probably going to perform basic first aid with some slightly advanced stuff thrown in. In a situation where you have a loved one who's in pain or bleeding or what have you, not everyone can stay calm. But if you have training, you're in a much better position to remain calm. So use that knowledge and save someone from pain or scarring or death. The more training you have, the higher you'll perform in an emergency situation.

As your kids grow up, include them. First aid and CPR classes can save lives. Even in a situation that's not as drastic, the classes give you knowledge, power, and perspective so there's not such a freak out moment.

You need to be calm and capable in times of injury. Knowledge can help with composure and making wise decisions. Accidents that tend to happen outdoors—broken arms, broken ankles, twisted knees, slips and falls, snake bites, bug bites, cuts—can usually be taken care of easily with basic first aid knowledge. Follow up care may be needed at an emergency room or with a doctor, but being prepared for the initial first aid is important.

HYPOTHERMIA IS DANGEROUS

We've talked about hypothermia in other chapters. When your body's core temperature drops it can be deadly. How you treat hypothermia is just as important as how you treat any other injury. Always take hypothermia seriously.

LET THE PERSON WITH THE MOST TRAINING BE IN CHARGE

If your spouse is trained in first aid, then your spouse should probably deal with the injury. If you are frantic, you are not helping anyone. If your child is screaming in pain because they broke their leg and your spouse is under control while making good decisions, stay calm. Don't add to the screaming. Don't bug your spouse while they're trying to focus on your child. If you're freaking out, the person who is providing the first aid is concentrating on two things—you losing it and actually dealing with the emergency. I suggest that if you're freaking out and you need a few moments to collect yourself, go for a walk or at least step away from the activity. Your child isn't going to remember that you stepped away for two minutes. The best thing for your child is to remove yourself from the situation until you're emotionally at a point where you can deal with it.

Also, if someone's in the middle of administering first aid, consider carefully what advice you give. If something's being done wrong and it's going to injure the person, then speak up. If they should be using the Barney band aid instead of the Micky Mouse band aid, then life is good and let them put the wrong band aid on. Just give the first responder room to treat the injured.

When there's an emergency, everybody needs to be clear-headed. Have a chain of command. Whoever is in the best position to provide care is in charge. Everybody else needs to support that person.

BE PREPARED

Sometimes the best help you can be is preparing things. While your spouse is administering first aid, a few helpful things you could do is gather wallets, identification, health insurance cards, snacks and drinks for the car ride, collect extra clothing and jackets for a short hospital stay. That way you're prepared for the admitting process at the emergency room and to stay overnight if needed. Think through what you'll need for the next 48 hours and get it all together while your spouse administers first aid.

KEEP THE SCENE UNDER YOUR CONTROL

If someone is freaking out and you are performing

first aid, you could divert their attention and ask them to do something meaningful by gathering the items I mentioned earlier.

There are times when Mom or Dad gets hurt, and with children around the situation becomes complicated. First off, manage the scene by corralling the kids into an area where you can easily see them. That way, if you need to apply pressure to a wound to stop a bleeding, you don't have to go look for the kids. If the kids aren't in your sight or they're running around out of control, then your attention is split and you're unable to provide the best possible care. This is where training your kids what to do in an emergency situation—who to call, where they are, what expectations you have of them—is imperative. With the children in place, you're in a better position to provide care. Having kids sit in a defined area and only help if you ask them is the best way to keep you from distractions and providing the best possible first aid.

BE PREPARED WITH FIRST AID SUPPLIES

Always have some first aid supplies at the campsite and a smaller subset in your pack. Some items—gauze for when someone's bleeding, a band aid for a cut, anti-itch cream for bug bites—are great to gain control of the situation.

After you assess the situation, stabilize the person. If you have to move them to more advanced care (i.e., a hospital) or get them in an ambulance, then the professionals are ready to make that transition.

WRAP UP

All these details come with training. There are plenty of first aid classes to choose from. It'll take a few hours in the evenings, but could save your life or your kids' lives or your wife's life. When you're outdoors and walking around in the woods, you are more likely to have an injury than when you are sitting on your couch watching television.

Being prepared to wrap a knee kept Connie moving on the Profile Trail on Grandfather Mountain

Training can save a life, and it might be yours. Be prepared and remember knowledge weighs nothing. Be prepared with first aid supplies. Don't forget that if something does go wrong, if you're having a hard time coping, sit down for a second. Because if you're the one providing first aid and your head isn't clear, then it's not in the best interest for you to continue at the moment.

This has been a tough discussion. You think you're just going camping. But the goal is to return home healthy.

Be prepared to administer first aid. Be ready to triage injuries. Know how to move someone injured to the next level of care if necessary, especially if you are far from professional help.

TWELVE

HIKING

You either hike to enjoy the journey or to get to your destination. Which are you?

When you're family camping, it really doesn't matter if you get to the end of the trail or not, because that's not necessarily your goal. One purpose is to have an adventure. The adventure could be a micro stroll of a hundred yards, or a hike of three miles. It could be six miles. It really depends on who's in the group, their physical fitness, and how interested they are in walking a long distance.

You may find you and your spouse have very different capacities for hiking. And that's just fine. You may find you like to work out and go hiking with your buddies and she goes hiking with you because you enjoy it. Now, if she doesn't work out and she's not used to climbing over rocks and walking over rough terrain, then she will tire quicker than you. I know one couple where the opposite is true. Addressing the comfort and capabilities of everyone in the group is critical to the success of your adventure.

WHAT MAKES A TRAIL DIFFICULT

The difficulty of the mileage depends on the difficulty of the trail. Several factors impact the difficulty rating. One is the trail conditions. If, with every stride, you're stepping over three-foot rocks, it's going to wear you out. Another is gaining or losing altitude. When you change altitude, your body has to work to raise your body up to that height. It's kind of like going up or down stairs. For example, you may gain five hundred feet in a mile. That may not seem like much, but it actually takes energy. If you're going to gain two thousand feet in a mile, that's going to take a lot of energy because it's very steep. So, you look on the map or the trail head and see how much altitude you're gaining or losing, and then decide. If you're hiking six miles and gaining a thousand feet, that's probably going to be a good workout.

Hiking Mount Mitchell - not for the faint of heart!

If you walk a half mile out and the same back, on a fairly easy trail (i.e., flat and no rocks to maneuver over) then most adults can knock that out and be pretty comfortable. But there again, if you walk a half mile and you gain four hundred feet of elevation, you're probably going to be breathing hard at spots. The difficulty of a trail is important to consider because you want everyone to feel success and enjoy themselves.

I'm providing these examples so you can have a basis for judging the difficulty of a trail. Most trails are graded by difficulty, distance, and elevation gain. Those three parameters give you a good idea of the effort involved in hiking the trail.

PREPARATION CAN MAKE A DIFFERENCE

If you don't like to hike much and you know a trip is in a month, I'd recommend you start walking to build endurance and strength. Consistency in the frequency of your workouts is the way to success. If you're not physically fit and you're not prepared, you're just not going to enjoy hiking as much. But if you start putting in twenty minutes a day and walk a mile a day at a brisk pace, you will feel a lot better hiking a month from now. This preparation gets you in better cardiovascular shape and builds muscle strength, which means you're less likely to injure yourself. So, even a small time commitment can make a big impact on your ability to enjoy the trip. If you are the only one to prepare then you are in a better position to lead the hiking and serve the rest of your family along the journey.

PHYSICAL LIMITATIONS

If you or somebody in your family has a physical limitation, you need to plan your trip around that. Park websites are loaded with information to allow you to plan as necessary.

INJURIES HAPPEN WHEN

Injuries happen in three circumstances: when people start to tire, during horseplay, and when the trail is in poor condition. Trails with snow or ice can be dangerous, as can slick rocks.

Back to horseplay for a moment, you have to strike a balance between actions with a low risk of failure and ones that could really hurt someone. If you fall off a cliff, many times you're dead. Therefore, it should be obvious to not let your kid's horse around near a cliff. On the other hand, if you fall on your butt while on the trail, you may not injure anything but your pride. Keep in mind that an injury two miles into a trail may require a team of people to extract the injured hiker.

THINK ABOUT WHO IS IN YOUR GROUP

If you have sixteen-year-olds in the peak of health and play sports, they're probably going to be waiting on you. That's why it's important which trails you pick. It's probably better to have a trail be a little short and then find another hike to do part of, or spend some time sitting at an overlook watching what's going on rather than beat yourself up on an overly difficult trail, saying "we have to get to the end of this trail" and making everyone miserable. The old adage "leave them wanting for more" is a sound goal when hiking.

Watch out getting on long trails, maybe greater than a mile, if you're not familiar with what your capabilities are. It is easy to say something like "it's just six miles", but sometimes six miles can be a long way. If you know what your abilities are, then you already know how far you can or can't go. If you don't know your capabilities, then keep it simple. If you have kids in tow, keep it even simpler. They're going to remember stopping to play in the creek as much as they're going to remember the trail you hiked.

Great trail near Blowing Rock, NC

DIFFERENT KINDS OF TRAILS

There are out-and-back, lariat, and loop trails. Out-and-back basically means you go to the end, you turn around, and you come back on the same trail. A lariat means you go and you keep walking but eventually the trail comes back to itself, and then you reverse direction and go back home. A loop is where the trail makes a loop; it may come back out near where you started, or it may return further away from where you started.

TRAIL MAPS AND REVIEWS

When you are considering a trail, make sure to read the reviews. Keep in mind the signature of the reviewer. For example, if someone loves hiking and their user name is HIKE_TO_LIVE, that will have a different connotation than someone named GRANDMA_FOR_LIFE. I'm not saying there aren't some grandmas out there in really good shape. But you can read between the lines and figure out the capability of the poster. One person's "easy" may be a triathlon's easy, versus someone who's not in good shape easy.

MOVE AT A COMFORTABLE PACE FOR EVERYONE

With individual differences that means you're going to end up setting the pace for one person. That's okay. You set the pace for that one person and then the rest of the time you smile, and you laugh, and you hope everybody else follows your example. That's how priceless moments are made. Whether or not you make it to the end of the trail does not matter. What matters is you return safely, and everyone has a great time.

If you're the one in good shape, you love to hike, and you're gung-ho, I'll caution you to temper your enthusiasm for where you're going and not put everybody else in a difficult situation.

DON'T PUSH ANYONE TOO HARD

If you push someone beyond their ability to perform at whatever level they can, then they may not enjoy this hike. They may not enjoy the rest of the day. Or they may slip and fall and hurt themselves. This is one of those times where kindness and love and joy can abound. And you just have to roll with the punches.

The point is to enjoy the day, no matter how easy the trail may be. Concentrate on your children's laughter and comments, and enjoy your time together.

SHOES FOR HIKING

Appropriate hiking shoes are imperative. This is where you're just going to have to make some decisions. If you're planning to hike miles, then your shoes need to protect your feet from the rigors of the trail.

I've got a pair of Asolo boots I've worn for years. It's my second pair of the same exact boot. When I wear these out I'll buy another. They aren't cheap, but the investment is worth it. Hiking boots and your waterproof jacket are the most important equipment for camping. Don't skimp on your boots if you are going to be hiking long distances. You'll want to take your time and find a pair that fit PERFECTLY. Stores like REI will take the time to make sure you have a perfect fit. Anything less is a fit you will regret on a long trail. Poor fitting boots can lead to nasty blisters. Back up your boots with hiking appropriate socks that wick moisture away from your feet.

Hiking boots will protect your feet from damage by rocks. Imagine you are stepping over uneven ground, if you're wearing tennis shoes they will conform to the rock which means your foot can only conform so far. This will lead to bruising, or worse you can hurt yourself. Whereas a hiking boot is somewhat stiff, so it provides a stable platform to keep your foot from having to try to bend and flex around obstacles. Trail running shoes are in-between a tennis shoe and a hiking boot. You may scoff, but your hard-soled work boots are good for hiking. In a lot of ways, they may be very similar to hiking boots. The point is to wear a comfortable shoe. If you're walking a half mile on a paved trail, then wear your tennis shoes. But in uneven terrain you'll need more stability.

Let's go back to the "But, it's our first camping trip, Montie," I know, you don't have to go to REI and spend hundreds of dollars.

A nice pair of new hiking boots will cost you between one and two hundred dollars. Or you could pick up a pair of barely-used Hi-Tec hiking boots for fifty dollars from Sierra Trading Post. You just have to decide where your budget and needs fall. I emphasize that if you will be car camping and not going on long difficult hikes, then make do with the shoes you have, assuming you won't be hiking over uneven terrain. You can upgrade later.

WHAT DO YOU NEED ON A HIKE?

When you're hiking, you need to have the right clothes. In other chapters we've talked about how to stay warm and dry. When you traverse more than a few hundred yards from the car, you need to have a jacket and some of the things we've previously talked about. This waterproof jacket is good for rain and to keep you warm. Remember, if you stay warm and dry, you stay alive.

Take bottled water to stay well hydrated and some snacks for energy. Be prepared with what you need to survive the night if someone becomes injured or lost. Getting wet, cold, and dying of hypothermia is a real risk in those situations. Many people have died of hypothermia when they got lost without realizing they were less than one hundred yards from safety. If you are on a trail and there is an injury, it may be several hours to a day before help arrives (depending on the location and how long it takes for help to arrive).

Give everybody a pack, or you carry a pack with everyone's stuff in it. Take a flashlight, just in case. Take a way for everybody to stay dry and warm.

If there's cell service, take your phone. If you don't have a hardcopy map of the trail, you can download it to your phone in case you lose service and get lost. Just keep in mind that paper maps always work, they don't have batteries to die and won't break when they are dropped or get wet.

STOP AND ENJOY THE VIEWS WHEN YOU CAN

Hiking allows you to go to a place you wouldn't otherwise go. While hiking, there are times when the trail and the view are beautiful. I'd encourage you to stop and take in the views, especially in the mountains where you have gorgeous panoramic vistas.

Amazing views off Blue Ridge Parkway

Stop. Sit. Chat. Laugh. Love. Wait for the priceless moment. It's not important to be focused on how many miles you've done, but instead spotlight the many smiles you've enjoyed.

You've hiked, you've burned calories, and now you're reaping the benefits in this beautiful, relaxing spot. Clouds go underneath you, or horses roam on the barrier islands of North Carolina, or whatever amazing sight you're at, just take it in. Leave your cares behind, this is your reward.

WHEN YOUR DAY DOESN'T GO ACCORDING TO THE PLAN

If you push everybody too hard the likelihood someone's going to slip and fall increases. A fall may make everyone in the group not enjoy the hike. They may not enjoy the rest of the day. Or if somebody twists an ankle and you get mad at them, they'll remember the moment of anger. This is one of those times where kindness and love and joy can abound. If your daughter twists her ankle and you have to carry her out, she will never, ever forget your kind actions. Twenty years from now she will recall how she twisted her ankle and her dad carried out. When that happens, twenty years from now that trail's going to be, like, six times as long. "It was seventeen miles my dad carried me out." I'm kidding about that. But, they're not going to minimize what you did for them. The story is going to grow, like a fishing tale.

Great day on the Profile trail on Grandfather Mountain

However, if she breaks her ankle, then her memory may be very different and she may never want to go hiking or camping again. Protect your family and your kids from injury. The trick here is if somebody does twist an ankle, smile, help them, and keep going. Get back to the car, drive to pick up some ice, make an ice pack with a Ziploc baggie. Don't look at it as ruining the day. Look at it as a family story. If someone falls and they get a boo-boo, well it turns into a story with value. These stories are told and retold. Make the day an adventure full of wonderful stories. They're not going to recall if they hiked one or four or six miles. What they're going to remember is how it felt to go hiking. They're going to recall the adventure. They're going to remember the conversation, the love. Those are the important things. And those are the things you can pull off.

ONLY DO AN EPIC HIKE WITH SOMEONE WHO *WANTS* TO AS WELL

If you want to do an epic hike, my suggestion is to find like-minded people! You may be lucky enough to have a spouse that wants to do that, but most likely not. Save it for a different time with a group of people who want that crazy-ten-miles-in-a-day-over-rough–terrain epic hike.

Just amazing to be here

EMERGENCIES

If you are ever in an emergency situation, its critical to remember if you're someplace like the top of a mountain (and this is especially true on tall mountains) your cell may be picked up from someone miles and miles away. So, you need to know where you are—what's the name of the trail, what's the name of the mountain, what's the name of the park—and communicate specifics, including the county and state you are in. That way the 9-1-1 operator can locate you quickly.

For example: I'm in North Carolina, in Mitchell County, on the Art Leob trail, because you may be talking to an operator a long way away. Make sure your kids know, and your spouse knows where they are. That way if something does happen and you're incapacitated, say you slip, fall, and hit your head, someone else in your party is aware of the details. Telling someone who's twenty miles away that you're in the middle of the woods on top of a big rock isn't going to get you help.

PLAN THE LENGTH OF YOUR HIKE

Make sure you have plenty of time to return to camp. Know what the weather's going to be and time getting back before dark. You don't want to be on a difficult trail trying to get back in the dark. It's a recipe for disaster. Finish your hiking by about three in the afternoon. On a safety note, that also increases the chance that someone will come along behind you, and if you're injured they'll be able to assist you.

SKILLS FOR CAMPING

EXAMPLES

There's a trail at Philmont, going up Mt. Rogers, they call the Thigh master. There were a lot of one to two foot, or even higher, steps. The terrain was uneven as were the rocks to climb the mountain, and you have a pack on your back. That was a pretty demanding trail even though it was probably less than a mile up.

Whereas, if you're hiking around Waccamaw Lake in North Carolina, where it's perfectly flat, you might walk a mile and not even notice it. You may just walk and talk and have a good time. And pretty soon, twenty-some minutes later, you've gone your mile. But, you'll find it's usually in between hard and strolling-easy.

Trail Markers

When you're in the mountains, normally it's a little more rugged. But there are times when you have trails that aren't. In the same park, some trails are rugged and some aren't. So pay attention to the maps and trail reviews.

A good example of opposites is at Linville Falls where you can take a paved hiking trail up to the top that is wheelchair and stroller accessible. Whereas if you go down and hike around the gorge, that's nowhere near stroller accessible. The lower path is always muddy. You have to step over slippery rocks. It's not a super difficult hike, but it's a lot more challenging than the upper trail that goes to the lookout above the falls. So, in the same area, you can have two very different experiences.

WRAP UP

Family camping usually isn't an epic adventure, but it can be cool. And it can be an adventure. Perhaps it even becomes epic because of the laughter and smiles, not because of the miles walked.

You'll find that hiking is a wonderful way to get around. You see things you wouldn't see otherwise and have a great time. Even if it's a half mile, or six miles, or maybe twelve miles — make the most of it. Enjoy the family time. These will be memories you keep and cherish.

It is way better to have a bunch of mini-adventures throughout the year than have a single epic adventure that may never happen. Enjoy those mini-adventures now.

THIRTEEN

BEAUTY FROM ADVERSITY

SOMETIMES OUR PLANS DON'T FOLLOW THE SCRIPT

Most times we envision what the weekend will look like, right down to the weather. But, even with our ability to read the weather radar and long-term forecasts, sometimes the meteorologists are simply wrong. When we expect something to happen and it doesn't, our response can make or break our good time and memories of the weekend. When things don't go the way you planned, facing the situation with a smile and a positive attitude helps lift everyone's spirits. Sometimes that can be tough to do in the middle of difficulties. However, the best stories and most meaningful memories often come from days when things didn't go as expected. How you respond to the challenge usually determines if it's a good or bad memory for all involved.

SKILLS FOR CAMPING

RISK IN OUTDOOR ADVENTURES

If you want to never get rained on, then don't leave the house. Never get snowed on, don't leave the house. When you go camping, there's a possibility that things might go sideways on you. It might rain. It might snow. It might be windy. The tent might leak. The car might break down. And I guarantee your car won't break down sitting in your driveway, not being used. So, as you go camping, you're putting yourself in a situation where there may be adversity.

CHOOSE YOUR ADVERSITY

If you're up for a hundred mile, two week backpacking trip, following the Rubicon Trail, go for it. If you're up for going to a park five miles away with your family, renting a camping spot, spending one night and coming home the next day to take showers, go for it. The trick is selecting the level of adversity that's going to work for you. And pushing yourself a little further the next time.

The amount of adversity is going to vary with different people. I work with a lady who grew up in California. As a child, they used to go horseback riding and then camp. They would bring their camping gear on their horses and ride on horseback to some awesome location. Then they'd camp there in the middle of a field. The next day they would ride their horses back. For them, that was a pretty wonderful trip and my friend has such great memories of these trips. But, apparently her daughter "would rather have a pitchfork stuck through her heart than to go camping." So, is she going to force her child to go on this tradition of a camping trip? No, she's probably not. It's a shame because her daughter is missing out on experiences because of a preconception and a bias, but that's between them. The important part is in this one family, you have a mother who would love to go camping and a daughter who doesn't think she'll enjoy it. The daughter won't allow any adversity in her life. Until she decides to embrace challenging circumstances, she'll miss out on some potentially wonderful opportunities. Now, is her life going to be ruined because she didn't go camping? Absolutely not. Could there be something added to her life experiences and her joy and her priceless moments? Yes. Is she going to miss those? Potentially? Yeah.

CHILDREN TEND TO FOLLOW THEIR EXAMPLES

If you are up for challenges and adventures, most likely your children will as well. If you start your children young, they'll have a better attitude towards these outdoor adventures. If you wait until they're teenagers, and it's a choice between them leaving all the comforts of home, including electronics, to go do something they've never done before, they may not want to go.

Take them camping when they're young and on a

regular basis. They can enjoy the process and won't be in that situation where they feel like they would "rather have a pitchfork through the heart than go camping."

FIGURE OUT THE LEVEL OF ADVERSITY OF YOUR FAMILY MEMBERS

This is probably under the heading of being gentle. You don't want to force feed someone something to the point where they totally reject it the rest of their lives. If you have a sixteen-year-old who doesn't want to go camping, but you do—then maybe you start out with long walks in the afternoon through the woods. Then day trips to hike in the mountains or see waterfall sights. And slowly work them up. Then, at some point, the next leap is overnight camping. Make it as simple as possible so it'll be a positive experience. Depending on your child or spouse, if they like horseback riding or ATV's, include that in the trip.

CHOOSE YOUR ADVERSITY BASED ON THE PLAN

Don't put someone in over their head to the point where they're totally going to reject it, because that's a fail all-around. If you take someone that would rather have a pitchfork through the heart than go camping, and you take them on a week-long trip, you've got three possibilities: one is they grumble the whole time but stick it out for the duration. The next is they love it and can't wait to go again. The last possibility is they hate it and you end up leaving early because everyone is miserable. Chances are low things will go well, so I'm not a big fan of forcing someone into a situation where they refuse to participate again for the rest of their lives. Instead, work them up and be crafty about how you do it. Don't deceive your kids, but have a plan. You're introducing them to something for their benefit.

TAKING IT SLOW MAY WORK OVER THE LONG-DISTANCE

You may be able to talk your kids into hiking or riding ATV's during the day and then staying at a hotel overnight. Maybe the activity they pick is a high-risk, high-reward one like ATV's or horseback riding. There's a thrill factor since you could fall off and possibly get hurt. But then you go back to a rental house or a hotel at night to ease them into the outdoor mindset.

If you are persistent, there's a good chance there's going to be a period in life about college where they have friends who want to go camping. They don't want to go camping, but they have a background with some experience. So, when a group of friends prepare to leave for a fun weekend of camping, your child may decide to finally give it a try. Your child has outdoors skills and attitudes to get them through so they will enjoy themselves.

If you wait too long, your child may never go camping,

but if you give them the skills, they may go as an adult. And then all of a sudden, later in life, you've got a camping buddy.

DIFFERENT LEVELS OF ENGAGEMENT WITH SPOUSES

If neither one of y'all want to go camping, then why are you reading this book? Unless you think, somewhere deep down inside, you want to try camping. Maybe it's on your bucket list. Or perhaps you have a group of friends who go. Maybe social pressure from said friends about being included in the group may push you over the edge. Understanding clearly the level of adversity and consciously choosing it puts you in a much better place to enjoy adversity during a camping trip.

FULL OR MICRO EXPERIENCES?

There are places you will never see when you stay at the Holiday Inn. For example, you can view the Grand Canyon from the observation bridge, or you can hike down in. There are places on that hike you'll never see from the North or South Rim. And maybe you're fine with that. So, it's not a matter of being Ted the Adventurer. These small, little micro-adventures are good, too.

You may have a mini-adventure on a weekly basis. You go canoeing one weekend; hiking the next. You go camping once a year, maybe even for only one night. And that's just fine. So, you just have to figure out what works. I suspect if you go camping yearly, at some point it'll become three or four times a year and that's awesome.

I want to prepare you so when you do make that decision, you're educated. The beauty is that knowledge weighs nothing. So, you can always take that with you.

WRAP-UP

You are safe in your house for the most part. But we have this beautiful land we live in called America and God's given us this amazing set of natural resources. And we can go enjoy them for low cost, almost no cost a lot of times.

Your life is richer, and you find those priceless moments when you go outside. You seek some adversity, you're prepared for it. You may get to the end of a camping trip and discover the adversity wasn't all that bad—because you were prepared. If you're not prepared, then adversity could be a really, ugly thing and that's not what we want for you.

The biggest part is testing yourself and teaching others to test themselves against adversity. That way they can become better, stronger people, ready for challenges outside of camping.

FOURTEEN

PLANNING FOR EXPECTATIONS AND EXPERIENCES

There are dynamics of expectations while camping. Let's break this down to get a handle on it.

EMOTIONAL ASPECTS

One is the awesome wonder of being outdoors and viewing the breathtaking sights and wildlife.

The second is natural, you're stressed because everything isn't as easy as it is at home. For example at home when you wash your hands and brush your teeth, your toothbrush and toothpaste are readily available. You turn the water on and brush your teeth, simple. Everything is right there. But when camping, it's very different because you have a toothbrush in a bag somewhere; toothpaste somewhere; water that's probably not with your clothes. You need to find all these things. You need to put your

SKILLS FOR CAMPING

shoes on to leave the tent and find the water. You have to find a spot where you can wash your hands and brush your teeth. You're carrying a towel and soap and your toothbrush and toothpaste and maybe a cup. At home this is a simple task, but it now becomes a time-consuming and complicated chore. The same goes for cooking or changing your clothes or a myriad of other things. Add that you may not have slept well because you're not in your usual comfy bed with air-conditioning and a perfectly regulated temperature. These normal everyday activities will add stress to your days and will accumulate. But read on and I will show you how to alleviate the tension and make these tasks less complicated.

Good food, good times, great smile

KEEP THE CAMPSITE ORGANIZED

When you pack, think about how you will unpack at the campsite. Bundle together common things so they are ready for use. You don't have to spend a whole bunch of money at REI buying a kitchen set-up or this or that. The more important part is to pack your gear the same way you will need it. You can pull out a box within a box, and all your "getting ready for bed" items are there. When I say box, I mean whatever element you are using to organize. I have some things in clear plastic containers with lids, other like items may be in canvas totes, yet others sit in buckets or bags. Use whatever containers work for you and the items you are bringing and using at the campsite.

I like to have a container for shoes set next to the tent. Every individual should have a small toiletries bag, so everything they need is self-contained.

SET EXPECTATIONS

Say you are the individual driving the camping trip. Generally, there's one person who's the most excited, who's going to make the arrangements and take care of everything. Probably that's you, the one reading this book. Consider the wide variety of expectations at home during a normal week. Those expectations are different with spouses and children of differing ages.

EXPECTATIONS AND KIDS

If you're the kind of person who wants to have your kids be your friends, you don't believe in discipline, and your kids run all over you, then this chapter's going to piss you off. I'm not apologetic about that because I want to help make your first camping trip a success.

Let's look at some polar opposites. One situation is

where your children are obedient and well-behaved—they understand they have a role in your family which involves getting up, working, and having a servant's heart. A servant's heart means if you see a need, you help out. Obviously, you don't want your two-year-old cleaning your gun or driving your riding lawnmower; that would be unsafe. But your 15-year-old may notice the grass needs to be mowed. Instead of ignoring the task or waiting to be told, he may go out and mow the lawn, assuming he knows how and has been trained to do it safely. I call this behavior the Boy Scout extreme. You know, being cheerful, thrifty, brave, clean and reverent.

The other extreme is the child with zero expectations placed on them. Sure they have some minimum amount of maintenance—they get up, brush their teeth, put on their clothes, eat breakfast, go to school, that type of thing. There are parents content with this situation in their home. If you're one of those, then listen up so your camping trip can be a success.

The reality is that no child is perfect, but I believe all kids have the ability to listen, obey, and help. Usually, they are somewhere in between.

SETTING EXPECTATIONS

Before you leave on the trip, take a few moments to consider what your expectations are for your child. If everything is done for them, they pretty much run the household by manipulation, and your friendship with your child is more important than being viewed as a strong authority figure, then the reality is when you go camping and you need someone to pick up firewood or help their mom with this, or help you with that, if they don't do it at home, why should you expect them to while camping?

Don't expect your children to go from undisciplined to disciplined simply because you're in a tent. I have bad news for you—that won't happen. They're going to behave the way they do at home. It's what they have been taught. It's their expectation.

I'm not preaching about how to raise your child, that's up to you. But I do think it is important to have realistic expectations. This book is about how to have an enjoyable weekend camping. If your child isn't helpful at home and whines and moans, they'll behave the same way camping.

On the other hand, if your child really wants to go camping then set appropriate expectations for them. They may never lift a finger at home, but now you have an opportunity to parent in a completely different environment so take advantage of it!

If your child doesn't want to go camping and is ill-behaved, consider thinking ahead and bribing. If the experience is successful, you'll go again and you can continue working on your child's attributes. You can buy a portable brick charger so they can keep their phone charged. Use the whole do-something-for-me-and-I'll-do-something-for-you trick. The goal is to create a positive experience for everyone. Make select compromises to bridge the gap between life at home and life camping. Find a middle ground that is a win-win for everyone.

LOOK TOWARD FUTURE TRIPS

Camping is a great place to jump-start a different parenting approach. Sometimes we find ourselves in a non-productive holding pattern. If your child likes camping, then each time you go you can push him a little further into less electronics and more helping. Give it a try!

WRONG EXPECTATIONS CAN RUIN A TRIP

Let's say you have an expectation. You're going camping and everybody's going to pitch in. Well, if they don't pitch in at home, and they won't empty the dishwasher, or fill up the dishwasher, then they're not going to wash dishes camping. Or if they do it's going to be with a lot of moaning and complaining.

Have a reasonable expectation of what to expect, based on people's past and recent performance at home, and come up with some ways to adapt. You can always keep breakfast real simple. Use paper products instead of plates you have to wash.

Think the weekend through. Talk it over with your spouse. How do you plan for success? How do you motivate? You have to figure out what works for your family.

WHAT IF YOUR KIDS DON'T WANT TO GO CAMPING?

If your kids are super helpful and highly motivated, they still may not want to go camping. They may just be city kids. And that's okay, because a lot of times people don't know what they're missing until they try it. So there again patience, loving, kindness—those are the elements of a successful weekend.

Your children have grown up with a certain level of expectations placed on them. You expect them to do certain things and behave a specific way. How you handle these things needs to be commensurate with the expectations you've developed over the long run. In this case, it may take a lot of adjustment on your part.

Sometimes, with kids, you have to ask them to trust you and give it a chance. Remind them they don't know everything. Experiencing life outside of their bubble may be a ton of fun, but they won't know until they try.

ELECTRONICS AND CAMPING

These days, even adults need constant entertainment. Even at work. I'm a mechanical engineer, I do product development. A lot of the times when I'm working on a project I listen to music or talk radio. When I'm at home I watch TV, or read, so there's a lot of entertainment in

SKILLS FOR CAMPING

One kid texting - one kid having fun

our lives. When camping much of that isn't possible. Batteries on phones die; there's no cell signal; there's no TV to watch. All of a sudden you've radically changed your day, probably replacing it with something much better, but it's a big change.

The electronic stimulus is replaced with the effort of camping. In order to enjoy the view you've got to stand there or hike somewhere. To savor the fire, you must build it. I'll argue you've replaced one thing with something much better. Years of conditioning are hard to replace in twenty-four hours.

When it comes to phones and electronics, make a decision. Everybody is so saturated these days that if you go totally electronic-free, it will be tough. Instead you can plan your day around some down time, so people can check emails or texts or play a game. Figure out what's going to work and set those expectations.

HAVE A SERVANT'S HEART

If you suddenly take away your teenager's phone, it's going to feel like punishment. So, you've got to occupy their mind. Let them ride an ATV through the woods in one of these guided trips, they'll forget about texting. But as soon as the ATV stops, the first thing they'll want to do is text because they want to tell their friends about their awesome experience. You may think, oh man, they're texting again. But that's a text you don't want to interrupt because they're reinforcing in their mind their joy of camping.

Whoever is leading this trip must have a servant's heart; they want to serve the people around them so everyone can have a memorable experience. A lot of times you lead through leadership as well as service. You may get up an hour earlier to organize the campsite because that'll make everybody's day go better, which ultimately helps you accomplish your goal. I encourage you to constantly consider how to keep the right state of mind to achieve your objectives.

EXPECTATIONS WITH SPOUSES

When it comes to your spouse—there are both men and women who are outdoor-oriented. You may not have married one. Your spouse may have zero interest in camping. Browbeating him or her into a trip is a risk. There are some people who simply won't camp. You're not going to get them to go. They might enjoy it if they did, but you can't force them.

The goal is buy-in from the spouse. He or she may tell you to take the children and have a good time because they want to go to the spa, or the car show. So you pack up the kids and go. There's nothing wrong with that. I've had camping trips where it was me and one daughter, or me and two daughters—and we had a wonderful time. It's okay if the spouse doesn't want to come.

Sometimes you can have a spouse that has no clue what they're getting into. Or perhaps they're scared of it. Or maybe they just don't like the idea. Arguing isn't what you want here. Assess their opinion and figure out what the tolerance level is. What is your spouse willing to do with the whole camping thing? The best solution may be to stay at the Holiday Inn but spend every weekend moment outdoors. Have an enjoyable meal somewhere. You've gotten outdoors, hiked, ridden an ATV, built a fire, all the things you wanted to do, but slept in the Holiday Inn instead of a campsite. And that's just fine, because you may discover the next time your wife is willing to sleep in a tent for a night. Grab the olive branch and make this trip the most glorious night.

With a hesitant spouse, ease them in slowly. Don't take them in November in the snow, wait until a mid-seventies weekend in September when you know for sure it won't rain. Keep them warm, keep them dry, keep them fed, and keep them happy. Work your way in.

She may never want to camp. It may always be just you and the kids, and that's okay. It doesn't have to be the whole family. I will tell you that I've had some wonderful camping trips with just me and the girls. The nice thing is that you can tailor a trip to whatever the group you're taking wants.

EXPECTATIONS WITH ACTIVITIES

My wife likes to sit by the campfire and read. Or enjoy the fire after dark and chat. She'll cook some while at the campsite, but her big thing is to hang out in her chair by the campfire. If I want to go hiking, she isn't interested and tells me to go on my own. She enjoys her thing and I enjoy mine, which is fine because at mealtimes we come together and in the evening we sit around the fire.

The goal is for everyone to have a good time. And if one party knows they don't want to hike, then that's fine. The point is to be together as a family for the weekend, but we don't necessarily have to do everything together. The nice thing is we know ahead of time what we will be doing, because we've talked and set the expectation.

Simple things can be memorable

SET YOUR OWN EXPECTATIONS

Avoid developing an unrealistic expectation that your teenager is suddenly going to become the world's greatest Boy Scout. Things are going to stay similar to how they are at home. But, there is a chance your kids and or spouse will absolutely adore camping. When they get into it, their whole demeanor could change, which is a massive win. But don't expect they'll fall in love because it may or may not happen.

WRAP-UP

I hope this has been helpful. I know it's hard to consider you are not doing a good job in this area. But that's okay. Sometimes camping trips are a journey of self-discovery, and the self-discovery is sometimes the most powerful part of it all. We may have to struggle a little bit and work a little bit. But then, all of a sudden, we discover more about ourselves. It might take a while to sink in, but it will definitely happen. Your kids are going to be discovering the outdoors as well as themselves. You may not see it, in fact they may not mention it until twenty years later, but it is happening.

FIFTEEN

CAMPING AT THE JEEP JAMBOREE

My wife and I packed up and headed to the third annual Jeep Jamboree at Uwharrie National Forest. I'm definitely looking forward to it. We'll spend two days on the trail and then part of the day participating in a driving course. And naturally we'll camp.

The Uwharrie Jeep Jamboree is a group of events that happen across the country. They are located in legendary locations like Moab, Utah, all the way down to awesome places like Uwharrie, in North Carolina. This event had a little over a hundred and ten Jeeps; eighty-one of them were participants with the rest as support vehicles or trail guides. They provide an opportunity for Jeep owners to gather and have a common experience, to go four-wheelin' together!

If you own a Jeep, you should consider going to a Jamboree. From what I understand, different Jamborees

SKILLS FOR CAMPING

Connie driving the Jeep

offer different levels of difficulty. There are some Jamborees with easy trails, and some where the easiest trails are a little more demanding.

WHAT DO YOU DO AT A JAMBOREE?

At the Jamboree you spend two-plus days on the trails. They're guided trips, so you've got support. If you break something, you've got a way to get back to camp. If you encounter a problem, you've got someone who knows Jeeps and can help. Also you've got spotters who help you through obstacles. Spotting is where someone guides you through a difficult obstacle because they can see exactly what your vehicle's doing, whereas you can't when you're driving it.

PACKING FOR THE JAMBOREE

We change our packing approach based on the needs of each trip. We camped in Arrowhead Campground in Uwharrie and spent most of our days trail riding in the Jeep. We pitched the tent, and since it is a developed facility with a bathroom, showers, and power, it's a little easier than when we go primitive camping.

This particular trip is a little more specialized because we've got the Jeep. Since we wanted options in case we broke something on the trail, we brought two vehicles. One is the Toyota 4Runner with our camping gear in it, and then the Jeep with the gear that we need for the trail trip.

We brought the 4Runner in case there's something we need for the Jeep—for example if we broke something on the trail. That way we've got an option for easily going back to town and not have to depend upon getting a ride somewhere. And also, the Jeep has practically no storage capability. So, it'd be tough to fit everything in there without making it a minimalist trip. And, a minimalist trip would mean no space for the giant tent my wife loves. We were also able to secure my tools and an air compressor in the 4Runner.

We opted not to use our Jeep hitch rack as we wanted the Jeep to be only for trail riding on this trip.

In the 4Runner, we've got a small air compressor to air the Jeep tires back up when we are ready to drive back home. We would have probably stopped at the Eldorado Outpost to do that, but because of the Jeep Jamboree, we thought there'd be a lot of people wanting to do the same thing. Anybody that didn't bring onboard air for their Jeep is going to want to go and air their tires back up before they head home. For those of you not familiar

Had to use a log to keep the wheel from coming apart after breaking an axle on a hill

with 4-Wheeling, on the trail you let air out of the tires and reduce the pressure to increase your footprint and increase your traction and to minimize the possibility of a rock damaging your tire.

WE BROUGHT A UTILITY TRAILER

So, we've got a 4Runner and towed a trailer. If we hadn't brought the air compressor then we wouldn't have needed the trailer, but the extra space makes packing easier. We're going an hour away; we're used to taking a trailer, so some other things I brought: a pop up ten-by-ten shelter, a plastic folding table, and a rake. That table has seen a lot of days of "glamping." I also brought some water. Even though there's water on site, this gives us five gallons of water right at the campsite. I brought some bottled water, too, which will end up in the Jeep.

So, the trailer's somewhat empty. And that's okay. There's really not a big gas mileage penalty when the trailer is lightly loaded. It's not a huge inconvenience, but packing up to leave will be quicker. Because, there again, Sunday morning, when we're headed back, the last thing I want to do is be forced to efficiently pack the 4Runner. This way I can put our boxes in the back and just head home.

FIREWOOD? FUNNY YOU SHOULD ASK...

We do have to provide a couple of our own meals. In

this case we either have to bring firewood or a stove. So, I brought a small backpacking stove. Making coffee for Connie in the mornings and warming up food for two meals is the main purpose of the stove. I've also got a Kelty pot in case I found twigs; maybe we'll use the Kelty pot. But that's very different for us because we normally build a campfire. To be honest, what happened was, when we left home I totally forgot to put any wood in the trailer and remembered when we were five minutes from the house! We decided to just keep going. We figured we'd probably be awfully busy with the activities from the Jamboree.

CAMPING LIGHT...FOR US

I took some of the things out of my camping box just to make it lighter and easier to handle, because we're not going to need them. I brought a hatchet, but I didn't bring an axe or the throwing axe. I took out the solar shower, since there's a shower at the campsite. And then the rest of the stuff—the lantern and the other things—I just left in the box. It wasn't important to unpack the whole box.

In some ways this is camping light for us. We are used to having the trailer, it has become convenient to just throw everything in the utility trailer.

This is a different trip and because some of the stuff was already boxed up, we probably brought more gear than we need, given the fact that the campsite provides showers and water and electricity. Since I had everything prepacked, I loaded up the trailer fairly quickly and hit the road. When I arrive home, we've segregated stuff that needs maintenance, like the tent and food boxes and so forth. Connie handles the food boxes, perishable versus not. When we return, one of the food boxes immediately goes into storage and the other she takes into the kitchen to clean out. We have a system.

IN PREPARATION, WE WORKED ON THE JEEP TOGETHER

I'm definitely looking forward to the Jeep Jamboree. This will be the first one we've ever gone to. Last weekend we actually did our first mod together to the Jeep; a little husband and wife "mechanicking." This is the first time we've worked on the Jeep together. That was kind of nice, especially getting ready for the trip.

GOING OFF-ROAD AT THE JEEP JAMBOREE

These events have a variety of drivers, from first timers like us, all the way to people who have done thirty Jeep Jamborees . . . I think the person who did the most was thirty-four. We've seen people at this event who spent the year travelling to events like this all over the country, going off-roading, which is really nice to be able to do that.

When you go to these events, you get an opportunity to do a lot of trail riding at the level you choose, based on your experience and equipment. I think it's important you know that when you go off-road, it's easy to break stuff. If "off-road" to you means driving across the backyard, okay, fine; you're probably not going to break much. But when you truly go on off-road trails, the likelihood of breaking something is a lot higher than normal. When you put your vehicle in a difficult situation, anything can happen. It's not an inexpensive hobby but is a lot of fun.

Line of Jeeps on the trail

HOW FANCY SHOULD YOUR JEEP BE?

The level of cost can be determined by several things. One is the vehicle. If you want to have the most-cool four-wheel drive on the planet, then you better have one heck of a budget. Optionally, if you want something where you can go out for the weekend, then build what you've got; or find a Jeep Cherokee and install aggressive tires and roll with it and lift it later. Keep in mind there are all sorts of things you can do to take the right vehicle. Some are fairly inexpensive, some are costly. I recommend not being so caught up in equipment. Just go and have a good time. You will find trails that are appropriate for the equipment

SKILLS FOR CAMPING

you have and later, if you want, you can add to that. There's a TV show called Dirt Every Day and that's kind of their mentality is to build something now and go enjoy it. Now, there are people whose enjoyment is building vehicles. They're hot-rodders, and there are people who do Jeeps that way. They take pleasure in designing how they're going to build up a vehicle. This weekend wasn't really about that. It was more about people who enjoy just being out on the trail.

MY THOUGHTS ON THE JEEP JAMBOREE

We had a great time at the Jamboree. For those of y'all that have never been to a Jeep Jamboree (which is most of the population), I'll make the argument go buy a used Jeep, go to a Jeep Jamboree, come back, clean up the Jeep, and then sell it—just to have the experience. That's how wonderful of a time we had! You learn so much about driving off-road. You're with a bunch of people who really enjoy being there. The trail guides are awesome and are avid four-wheel drive guys. So, it's kind of the love of being outdoors, but in a Jeep.

Lot of Jeeps

On these events, if you pick more difficult trails, you

do run the risk of breaking stuff. At one point the back of the Jeep slammed the spare tire into the ground going across a really ugly ditch. That was mostly my fault for not braking down the back side of the ditch. On a lot of Jeeps, you'll see the spare tire on the back, and it's perpendicular to the ground when it comes from the factory. Well, mine is not quite perpendicular now; it's a few degrees off. But, you know, I'm probably the only one who notices. And the back gate no longer shuts perfectly. But, hey, as long as it seals, that's okay with me. Jeeps that go off road develop "character" that way.

A LITTLE JEEP JAMBOREE STORY

So, we got a little scar on the Jeep, but it's a great story and was definitely worth the experience. At one point we were waiting at the bottom of a hill with a nasty climb ahead of us. I knew there was a potential for a high penalty for failure. While we were sitting there, I was debating about whether or not I'm going to go around the hill. And my wife, my wonderful, wonderful wife said, "You know, the Jeep's insured, if you break something we'll fix it on Monday." (If you're my insurance agent, you didn't hear any of this.) She said, "We need to go up this hill and we need to have a good time doing it." Now, I will say on this particular hill, I didn't make it all the way to the top. I had a little bit of an issue almost at the top. And so, we had to go back. We stopped and got some help and winched the Jeep up the hill. There was a little tight spot when I thought I was either going to leave the fender or a mirror for a second, because of a tree that was in an inconvenient spot. But, we got away from there without doing any significant damage. I don't know if that mirror will ever be completely straight again. But, you know what? It is not a big deal. We had a great time. The Jeep has even more character now. It was worth it. Having Connie encourage me along the way made the time even sweeter. Priceless moments.

SET FOR SUCCESS

I think a lot of things set us up for success. One was that Connie does a wonderful job keeping us organized when we're camping—getting us ready, organization-wise. So, we'd climb into our tent at night; the tent was clean; there's a place for dirty shoes; the bed was comfortable; and the bedding was appropriate for the weather. It was dry. She had all this worked out and we even played cards one night. We were sitting around on the air mattress playing cards and having a wonderful time. Our first Jeep Jamboree was a roaring success.

SIXTEEN

PHYSICAL FITNESS IMPROVES CAMPING EXPERIENCE

Part of the problem with tents is that as you grow older, getting in and out of them proves to be more difficult. As we age, our mobility and flexibility decreases. You may tire of sleeping directly on the ground, even if there is a mattress there.

CONSIDER YOUR SEASON OF LIFE WHEN SELECTING SLEEPING ACCOMMODATIONS

If you have something like an RV or a teardrop trailer (which we discussed in an earlier chapter) your mattress is at a more appropriate height. Keep in mind that as time progresses, your needs may change. As we age, our body's less resilient. Be sure to make accommodations so you continue to be comfortable and have fun camping.

TAKE CARE OF YOURSELF SO YOU'LL ENJOY CAMPING MORE

Camping keeps you busy and is hard work. If your body is not in good shape and you haven't taken care of yourself, then you're not going to enjoy camping as much because your body's less capable and less adaptable. Hey, maybe I'm stepping on toes and that's fine. But, when we start talking about these adventure type things like overlanding, I think it really does bring up the concept of more rigorous trips. We also discussed hiking. But even just regular camping, if you've taken the time to invest in yourself to make sure your body is physically healthy, then you're ahead of the game when you camp because you'll enjoy your time more and deal less with being tired or sore.

BECOME A FAN OF REGULAR EXERCISE

To achieve a healthy body, get on a regular exercise program. I joined a boot camp fitness class, which has been awesome. It takes thirty minutes, three times a week, and the impact on my quality of life has been substantial. I don't have to go to the gym three hours a day, just thirty minutes three times a week. Occasionally I'll miss one. But I don't miss a whole lot of classes and it works well because I've worked it into my schedule. At a certain time,

I leave to go to class and my wife knows what time I'm coming back. It's simply part of our life now.

Most people don't have the discipline to go to the gym, even if it is only three times a week for thirty minutes. One way to get around that is to find a class you are interested in that costs money. If you're paying money to do something and it's tied to an event, you're likely to go. If it's tied to a gym membership with no accountability, you put it off. I know with an event, at least for me, I feel pressure to fulfill my commitment. I plan my schedule around the activity.

Before I started this exercise program I weighed much more than I do now, and when I exerted myself I'd be tired. It was no fun. Regular exercise has gotten me to where exertion during camping or outdoor activities is enjoyable now, because I'm not exhausted all the time!

SEARCH FOR AN EXERCISE YOU WILL STICK WITH

So, a thirty minute boot-camp class has changed my life, what will motivate you? Joining a health club with a friend for accountability? A fast-paced walk in the neighborhood or a local park on a regular basis? Walking on a treadmill or elliptical in the basement while you stream your favorite television show on your phone?

Find something that works for you, that you are able to do consistently. Be patient. It may take a few tries to find the activity that motivates you to get physically fit.

CONSIDER CHANGES IN DIET

Having this change in exercise put my body in a better physical condition and allowed me to enjoy camping and outdoor activities without feeling tired or overly sore. I've also made changes in my diet. Now, I'm going to be the first one to admit that I love Bojangles. And I'm not advocating any particular diet plan or telling you how to eat. I'm simply sharing some things that helped me with enjoying camping trips and being outdoors. Some of the things we've done is cook nutritious meals for dinner. My wife also started packing my lunch. Now, I am very blessed to have a woman willing to pack a meal for me. Because I'm eating fruit or crackers and cheese or maybe some salami or something instead of chips from the machine, or what have you. So, lunch and dinner are pretty doggone nutritious. We dine out once, maybe twice a week. So, Friday's the cheat meal and I eat what I want. And that's fine. I found if I get up and cook my own breakfast, I tend to eat more nutritious than if I just run by Bojangles.

Are there ways you can modify how you eat? Cut out carbohydrate and sugar-filled snacks. Add in fruits and vegetables. Eat in more and out less. Make the cheat meals fewer and the healthier ones more abundant. Keep in mind that "every meal doesn't have to be a party in your mouth" as Chris Tolp with Isotolp in Apex, NC, is fond of saying.

SIMPLE THINGS CAN IMPROVE YOUR QUALITY OF LIFE.

For me, these elements have improved my quality of life, and made a lot of activities more enjoyable. You're going to make your own decisions. You're an adult, you're reading this. I'm not telling you that you have to change things. I am saying if you want to enjoy these experiences with your children and with your wife or your husband, being in better shape means you're less grumpy, you're more prepared, and you're going to smile easier.

If you're tired and worn out, it's hard to smile, hard to have fun. If you're not so exhausted, you're well rested, and your body's better treated, then all of a sudden, you find those priceless moments easier. I know when I get tired and grumpy, that is a priceless moment killer. But when I stay in good shape and eat healthier, then my weight stays down and I feel better. It's true for all of us. What changes can you make?

SEVENTEEN

CAMPING AT DIFFERENT STAGES OF LIFE

I camped when I was young and single, then as a family, then as a married man with my spouse at home, and with kids after I was divorced. There were times I've taken one or both kids and we've gone camping for the weekend without mom. Because of these different circumstances, I wanted to hit on camping with kids when you're just you and the kids, camping as a single person, and camping as married but your spouse isn't with you and maybe the kids are, or the kids aren't.

SOLO CAMPING

I like to go hunting. Sometimes I'll hunt with a group, but the vast majority of the time I go by myself. I usually make a yearly trip to the mountains for a few days. My kids are adults doing their own thing in different parts of

SKILLS FOR CAMPING

the state. My wife is supportive of this trip as she doesn't like to hunt. So, when I go hunting, I camp. I set up base camp, which for me means simple car camping. In the early morning, I'll leave to hunt and later come back. One thing that becomes really obvious after you've camped as a family is that when you're camping by yourself, it's a lot more work. You've got roughly the same amount of things to do but you've got one person doing them.

PACK ONLY THE NECESSARY ITEMS

When solo camping, it is very important to pick and choose what you really need. What do you need to be comfortable? What can you live without? You don't want to have a bunch of equipment to deal with that isn't relevant to a solo trip. You may have "just in case" equipment that stays in the car and doesn't cause an inconvenience. If the weather's nice, maybe you don't put up a shelter for your kitchen, it stays in the car. Or there may be something you thought you needed, but found out you didn't.

Even though this is a solo trip, you may be meeting some guys, which means a bunch of people pitching in and sharing shelters and utensils and all. Also, if you're camping alone, then you need to plan around that. What kind of activities do you want to do? It's easier in a way because it's just you deciding what you want to do.

SECURITY

If you've got a group of people, you're less likely to be a target than if you're a single woman out in the woods. There are a lot of women that safely make it down the trail every year. Consider what you would do if all of a sudden you found yourself in a bad situation, and plan for that as best you can. You can prepare for that by having a defensive weapon that helps you protect yourself.

DEFENSIVE WEAPONS

Defensive weapons can range from bear spray all the way up to carrying a firearm. If you decide to carry a firearm, there are different state and national laws. So, you'll need to check. If you're in a park, you'll need to check with the laws for that park. A lot of parks want you to carry concealed if you carry a firearm. Most states you have to have a permit to do that.

If you choose to carry a firearm, you'll want to train so you know how to use it. And then, the other thing is you want to make sure you understand the laws of where you're going and where you're passing through, because some states don't offer reciprocity. That means your conceal carry permit from North Carolina, for example, isn't valid in Maryland. Be aware.

Now, if you're going camping in a month and you've never fired a firearm, go for the bear spray. You need to have time to prepare, learn, and get yourself up that curve of shooting. If you've got six months and you have time to take some classes and learn how to do it right, get your conceal carry permit, because it's a valid way to protect yourself.

Don't let the fact that you're single keep you from camping, but do think about what to do if you're attacked and how you can prevent an attack. There are tons of self-defense classes that you can avail yourself with.

TIME AWAY CAN BE A GOOD FOR YOUR SPIRITS

Sometimes having time away from your normal routine and changing your context is healthy. If either spouse wants to get away for a few days, that's not a bad thing. If they're comfortable being outdoors and they've got some outdoor skills, then it's less to worry about.

CAMPING WITH YOUNG CHILDREN, SOLO ADULT

If you have a situation where you're taking your young kids, and you'll be the only adult on the trip, it's more work than a solo trip. Let's say you've got eight-, nine-, ten-year-old kids. While camping, you're going to be doing all the work needed to run the site, and you're going to be taking care of the kids. It's important to keep that in mind when you plan activities or where you're going. Think about how much time you want to sit around the camp versus getting up and doing physical activities with your children.

For several reasons, you may want to stay closer to home. You may want or need to go home because you or one of your children gets sick injured. It's easier knowing you are a short drive back to the safety of your home. Or perhaps one of your kids gets homesick and wants to go home. The other consideration is the drive length, the shorter it takes to get there, the shorter drive you'll have on your way home.

CAMPING WITH KIDS, FIND THE RIGHT BALANCE

With taking care of the kids and setting up camp, you should set yourself up with a great chance of success. That way, you've got a little bit of time to relax with the kids as you're setting up camp; maybe choose a campground with a bathhouse. It's important to find what I call a work/joy balance. Make sure you have time to do stuff with the kids. If you take on too many activities or make the camp set up difficult, then you may not find that balance. A long drive tires you out. Not having convenient facilities with little ones sets yourself up for failure. Put yourself in a situation where everyone is comfortable. Consider meals at a local restaurant instead of over a campfire. Keep it simple and I promise it'll pay great dividends. The goal is to make everyone want to go on another camping trip in the near future.

SKILLS FOR CAMPING

FIRST CAMPING TRIP AFTER A DIVORCE

If you're recently divorced or separated and you take your kids camping and this is your first trip, then there are some extra things you need to consider. After a divorce or during a separation is one of the great tragedies of life.

A lot of times you've got someone who takes their kids camping who may really be hurting. When you go camping, you take a situation where you're working harder than normal, because you're taking care of the kids, you're taking care of the camping stuff; but you're hurting. And so now, you've got the baggage that you're packing up and putting with your camp stove. The challenge is to take that baggage and leave it in the car or leave it at home because you've got this opportunity to take your kids on this great weekend. Don't ruin it for everyone by complaining about the ex or behavior that is just inappropriate somehow, because you may ruin your kids from camping. They may never want to go again because they saw this weekend that Dad or Mom was in such pain. Or all they did was complain about the other parent.

Don't take an opportunity to have these wonderful moments with your children and throw it away. I'm being very direct here in how I'm describing divorce and emotions. But I believe it's valid because I've been through it. There were tough periods, but don't let those feelings bleed into your time with your children. It would be a shame to miss out on something that's low cost and that you can enjoy. This can be a time to get away from it all, change the context, and spend time with your kids the way they'll remember for the rest of their lives. Seek out those precious moments.

CAMPING WITH ONLY ONE CHILD

Don't ever underestimate the value of one-on-one time with your children. Let's say you've got three kids and even if you're an involved parent—you're attend all the soccer games, you're at piano recitals, you're sitting on the porch every night—I'll make the argument that your child would probably love to have time with just dad and the kid. One kid, one dad; or one mom, one kid.

Special one-on-one time with your children can be a really wonderful time and create special memories. It's a little more work, just you and one child. But, it's a time that you're out of the context and there's just the two of you. The memories you make will get brought up thirty, forty years later around the kitchen table. It may not seem like it at the time, but it will.

ALCOHOL AND CAMPING

If you are the only adult camping and you've got your kids, be practical and leave the alcohol at home. If something unexpected happens, that could be anything from a bear in the campsite to a person walking through your campsite to somebody twisting an ankle or somebody wanting to go home in the middle of the night, you're the responsible one. Also, you can get in a lot of trouble for drinking at a lot of these campgrounds.

WRAP-UP

This gives you some phases of life that not all of us go through but many of us do. I hope some of my experiences will help you during your camping trips. In general, happiness equals the appropriate amount of work, which you can adjust by where you camp, what amenities are available, how much stuff to bring, what activities you're going to do, and so on. Security is always something to keep in the back of your mind.

When you start looking at camping this way and compromising, then all of a sudden it's easier to make good decisions about a successful camping trip.

EIGHTEEN

CAMPING WITH A DOG

Everyone is used to having their family dog around. Perhaps he sleeps at the foot of the bed every night or in your bed or your kid's bed. Your dog is family. Do you take him camping with you? Let's talk through the pros and cons and look at some tips on how to make bringing your dog a success.

CAMPING IS MORE WORK THAT YOUR USUAL ROUTINE

At a campsite, a lot of non-typical stuff happens and most activities are tiring. Let's take dinner for example. You are cooking over a fire that you've worked to build for over an hour. There is no usual kitchen table. Everything is more labor and thought intensive because you are in a completely different environment. If you've brought the dog, you have an additional responsibility.

You're busy with your new routine, and the dog is one more thing to draw your attention away from making special memories with your children. Caring for him in a campsite scenario may create undo frustration.

YOUR DOGS' INTENTIONS DON'T ALWAYS MATCH THE FAMILY PLAN

If we take the dog with us, we tie him to a central spot with plenty of leash or rope. We humans think life's good. Except, what happens when he spies a squirrel or gets tangled up with his leash? Your dog may not find this situation enjoyable.

Conversely, what if a snake slithers by or a coyote eyes your pup? Your dog is now in danger.

WHAT TO DO WITH YOUR DOG AT THE CAMPSITE

What happens if you don't tie your dog up at the campground and he runs away? Well, it depends. He may be back in thirty seconds. I have friends whose dog stays right there. Now, they live on a farm so the dog's used to going around with them all day. He has learned the concept of staying in the general area with his owners. Except most of us live in the suburbs and probably can't do that. You take your dog out on a leash or let them into a fenced backyard. Dogs these days have no idea how to fend for themselves. When you go camping, you can't expect your dog to suddenly know what to do if it's free to roam around. So to make sure he doesn't get away you need to keep him on a leash, except now you've got one more thing to manage.

YOUR DOG IS AT RISK

If your dog is outside tied up and you leave the campsite for a few minutes, he is susceptible to being attacked by other predators, even if you have a big dog.

If you are with him and a rabid animal, like a raccoon or coyote, is around, your dog is a target and could get bit or mauled. Or perhaps he gets bit by another dog that's loose.

Either way, this means an emergency trip to the vet, likely in a strange town or possibly having to go home, depending on how bad the wounds are. There are a lot of scenarios you can't predict on a weekend that's already unpredictable.

Another thing to consider is that if your dog eats something poisonous, or feces from another animal, that can make him sick. Now you have a dog that's not feeling well so you're paying attention to him rather than creating those wonderful family moments.

AN UNTRAINED DOG OFF LEASH AT A CAMPSITE

If you let him off leash and he scrambles after a squirrel and either gets lost or simply ignores your calls, you have a problem. Perhaps a coyote or another dog at the campsite chases him, which is another problem. Maybe your dog is overzealous and runs up to people at other campsites, annoying them and creating tension for the weekend.

If your dog runs away, you are now spending your weekend searching for him. You have gear and little ones to look after, and you've got to find your dog. Your situation becomes trying and you've only just arrived! You don't need that kind of stress on your first camping trip, leave the dog at home or with a trusted friend until you have some experience under your belt.

A WATCHDOG TYPE OF DOG

If your dog has a watchdog mentality, then every time something moves outside he may bark or growl or grow anxious. About the tenth time you're woken from peaceful slumber by barking at a deer or skunk or bear, will be the moment you realize you shouldn't have brought the dog. Of course, it's hard to know how he will behave sleeping in a tent if he's never experienced that before.

Our previous dog, Zena, would watch everything while she was awake. But when we got in the tent and she went to sleep, she pretty much didn't stir for the rest of the night. She didn't bark much anyway unless she perceived a threat. She barked very little at the campground and was a great dog to camp with.

SOME DOGS ARE BARKERS

If it's 3 a.m. and your dog's pitching a fit, especially if

you're in a campground with a bunch of other people, you may have a problem to deal with. You might have to take the dog home in the middle of the night. The best way to stay out of that situation is to leave him at home.

One option is to camp on your property. That way you're not out a ruined trip because the dog kept everyone up. Pitch a tent in the backyard; put the dog in the tent; roll over and go to sleep and see what happens. It gives you a good chance to check out your gear, and at the same time see how he does in the tent. If you're not used to sleeping on the same level with the dog, then that may or may not be a problem. Zena, she slept five feet away; life was good. I know other people with dogs that like to climb in bed with them.

BE CONSIDERATE OF OTHER PEOPLE

If you're in a campground, other people are close by. People may want to play with your dog when they first see it, especially if children are in the next campsite. Except, there is risk involved. What happens if one of the kids does something to the dog and he bites them? Now your weekend is really ruined. You may deal with the legal ramifications of that for a long time.

THE PERFECT DOG STILL TAKES EFFORT

Let's say you have a dog that stays right where you are and never runs off. Or is content tied up. You've done what you needed. The dog's happy. Except you need to feed him, make sure he gets exercise, and take him away from his tied up area to use the bathroom. On a weekend that is already packed, that may be too much to deal with.

On the other hand, we were four-wheelin' with a guy in February who took his dog four-wheelin' with him. When he got to a difficult section with a rollover possibility and he didn't want the dog to be at risk, he would command the canine to get out of the truck. The dog would jump out and run ahead to meet his owner at the next intersection of trail. The dog knew not to get in the way of any of the Jeeps. This situation is unique because the owner knew his dog would not chase after wildlife or run away, but that he'd obediently be waiting for his master after the obstacle.

THERAPY DOG

The only time I would be more in favor of taking a dog on a first camping trip is if you feel he will help one of your children deal with camping better. Maybe your child is very attached to the dog or is anxious about the trip but all of a sudden isn't anxious if the dog can come. That's a call you have to make. Are you being manipulated to bring the animal? Would it truly help your child if the dog came? Those are questions you must answer as a parent.

HAVE DOG WILL TRAVEL

If you bring your dog and want to leave the campsite, you can't. You must take him with you. This can be problematic in a couple of ways. Let's say you decide you want to go for a five mile hike. Well, the dog I have right now laughs at a five mile hike. She's totally ready to go. But our previous one, as she got older couldn't go that far anymore. Now, if we want to go for a hike, we're constrained by the dog with us.

Let's say you decide to run out for lunch or dinner, or you need to go to the store. You can't bring a dog into a lot of these places. You also can't leave him in the car in hot weather. Say its seventy degrees outside, you make the call to run into the grocery store with the dog in the car. Some do-gooder decides it's too hot in your vehicle and next thing you know, they're breaking out your window to rescue your dog from overheating. It's legal, and now you have a broken window to content with. Or, say its eighty-seven, you park in the shade and the windows are partly down, it's really not that hot in the car, but state, city, or county ordinance states that above a certain temperature a law enforcement officer is obligated to remove the animal from the vehicle. Now you're looking at a potential charge of abuse and neglect. You've got a two-hundred-fifty dollar window that's now gone. There's glass all over your car. There's a really good chance that at this point, you're packing up your car and going home, but first you need to get out of jail.

A SINGLE PERSON AND THEIR DOG

If you're single, then some of these things become bigger issues because you don't have anyone to leave the dog with if you need to go into the store or if you want to go out to eat. On the other hand, you may have brought your dog for protection because he might dissuade someone from threatening you or worse. The decision is up to you.

CONSIDER THE PHYSICAL CAPABILITY OF YOUR DOG

My neighbor has a small, ankle-biter, yet sweet pocketbook dog. We all know he will not go on a two-mile hike, unless you carry him. If your dog is physically not capable because of age or health or just because he is too small to walk a long distance, then you're activities are constrained. You're not going to have an impromptu hike if the dog can't go.

INVEST IN A BACKPACK FOR YOUR DOG

If your dog is physically capable of carrying their own water, consider a doggie backpack, that way you don't have to carry their things. You can put food, water, and collapsible bowls in them.

Your dog needs water just like you. Depending on the situation, he may be even more sensitive to running out of water than you are. Carry water for your dog if you're away from camp and make sure he has plenty of water when you're at the site.

The dog we have now can easily carry her own supplies, which makes my pack lighter.

LEAVE THE DOG AT HOME FOR YOUR FIRST CAMPING TRIP

For your first trip, leave your dog at home. You can board him, hire a sitter, or drop your pooch off with a neighbor.

A lot of the boarding places are wonderful.

Your dog will have a good time. He will miss you, but will have fun and play with other dogs, kind of like a vacation. The big issue is cost. Also, he needs to be up to date on his shots.

There's a lot of experience behind my opinion. I don't want to see your first camping excursion become a disaster because you brought the dog and had issues.

I'd encourage you to consider these things as you decide whether or not to take your pet. I look at it as a risk-versus-reward. On your first trip, I don't see the reward. Later on, absolutely, bring the dog and have a good time. By then you'll know much more about camping and what to expect.

FOR THE READER

Thank you for buying and reading *Skills for Camping* (Montie's Guide to Camping, Book Two). I truly hope you were able to learn from my experiences and make your most recent camping trips even better than before! Camping is a gateway to family fun in the outdoors. Enjoy the hiking, views, and all the special moments you and your loved ones share.

If you enjoyed *Skills for Camping* (Montie's Guide to Camping, Book Two), please review it on Amazon and Goodreads. You can keep up with what is going on in the outdoor world in North Carolina by visiting:

www.montie.com

You can find out more about my books at:

www.montie.com/books

If you haven't read my prior book, *Family Camping*

(Montie's Guide to Camping, Book One), feel free to grab that in either Kindle or print format. Here's a quick blurb:

> Written for beginner to semi-seasoned outdoor-enthusiasts, this book will not only teach you how to camp but show you what to expect, how to plan activities, and how to create traditions. The word "camping" inspires smiles in many people. Learn how to escape your daily life and create memorable family experiences in the woods.

Thanks again for letting me share our outdoor adventures with you!

www.ingramcontent.com/pod-product-compliance
Lightning Source LLC
Chambersburg PA
CBHW052032070526
44584CB00016B/2011